Signs
of Life

Signs of Life

The Letters of Hilde Verdoner-Sluizer from Nazi Transit Camp Westerbork 1942—1944

Hilde Verdoner-Sluizer.

Edited by her daughters
Yoka Verdoner and Francisca Verdoner Kan

Foreword by Jacob Boas

ACROPOLIS BOOKS LTD.
WASHINGTON, D.C.

DS
135
N6
V47
1990

ACROPOLIS BOOKS LTD.
Kathleen P. Hughes, Publisher
11250-22 Roger Bacon Drive
Reston, Virginia 22090

Attention: Schools and Corporations
ACROPOLIS books are available at quantity discounts with bulk purchase for educational, business, or sales promotional use. For information, please write to: SPECIAL SALES DEPARTMENT, ACROPOLIS BOOKS LTD., 80 SOUTH EARLY STREET, ALEXANDRIA, VIRGINIA, 22304

Are there Acropolis Books you want but cannot find in your local stores?
You can get any Acropolis book title in print. Simply send title and retail price. Be sure to add postage and handling: $2.25 for orders up to $15.00; $3.00 for oders from $15.01 to $30.00; $3.75 for orders from $30.01 to $100.00; $4.50 for orders over $100.00. Virginia residents add applicable sales tax. Enclose check or money order only, no cash please, to:
ACROPOLIS BOOKS LTD.
80 South Early Street
Alexandria, Virginia 22090

"The Lost Pearl" by Susan Kan is printed by permission of the author. The poem also appears in *Bubbe Meisehs by Shayneh Maidelehs; an anthology of poetry by Jewish Granddaughters about Our Grandmothers.* Edited by Lesléa Newman. Published by HerBooks 1989. Santa Cruz, California.

The passage on page 222 from *In Dépôt* by Philip Mechanicus. Copyright © 1964 by Polak & Van Genep, is reprinted by permission of Uitgeverij en boekhandel Van Genep.

The editors would like to acknowledge the following translators: Jacob Boas, Jolanda M. de Levie, and Lettie S. Multhauf; and Tilia Klebenov for the Time Line.

Library of Congress Cataloging-in-Publication Data
Verdoner-Sluizer, Hilde, 1909-1944.
   Signs of life: the letters of Hilde Verdoner-Sluizer: from Nazi Transit Camp, Westerbork, 1942 to 1944/edited by Yoka Verdoner and Francisca Verdoner Kan.
      p.   cm.
   Includes bibliographical references.
   ISBN 87491-955-X: $18.95
   1. Verdoner-Sluizer, Hilde, 1909-1944—Correspondence. 2. Jews-Netherlands—Correspondence. 3. Holocaust, Jewish (1939-1945)-Netherlands. 4. Westerbork (Netherlands: Concentration camp) 5. Netherlands—Ethnic relations. I. Verdoner, Yoka, 1934- . II. Kan, Francisca Verdoner, 1937- . III. Title.
DS135.N6V47   1990
940.53'18'092—dc20   89-80035
                                                  CIP

For
Jeanette
Susan
Elly
Gerry
David
and
Rachel

Contents

My foes have snared me like a bird,
Without any cause.
They have ended my life in a pit
And cast stones at me.

Lamentations of Jeremiah (3:52)

Foreword

"I try not to reflect; that is absolutely futile, and I cannot envision any plans for the future at all at the moment. I just float, at least for the time being," wrote Hilde Verdoner-Sluizer in January 1944.

"Floating"—it would be difficult to think of a better word to describe the nature of the place that produced this state of mind: Westerbork. For Westerbork, a Nazi transit camp in the Netherlands, was a human warehouse whose Jewish inventory was on hold until such time as the "Final Solution" necessitated its further "processing" in the East. In the course of roughly two years, from July 1942 to September 1944, ninety-three trains dispatched some 105,000 of Holland's 140,000 Jews to their deaths in the annihilation camps in Poland. Of those, no more than 5,500 lived to tell about it.

Among the victims was the author whose letters appear in this volume, Hilde Verdoner-Sluizer. Hilde, to use the name with which she signed her letters, was taken to Auschwitz in a cattle car on the eighth day of February 1944, a month after she penned the lines cited above. "My worst fears have been realized," she wrote to her father, also in

Westerbork, on the day before she was deported, "and I have been called up for transport. Do what you can! I have very little hope." Hilde was gassed on February 11. She left behind a husband and three small children, all of whom survived the war in hiding.

Born on November 28, 1909, in Amsterdam, Hilde Sluizer grew up in a middle-class family and received a good education, excelling in languages. After graduating from high school and a two-year course in homemaking, she went to study Italian in Perugia, then to Rome to take a job as a secretary, a job she would also hold in Westerbork. Mussolini was in power, and, ironic as it may seem in retrospect, the changes effected under his leadership appear to have impressed her favorably. Back in Amsterdam, she fell in love with Gerrit Verdoner and married him on December 12, 1933.

After their marriage, Gerrit and Hilde moved to Hilversum, a residential suburb in the heart of Holland. There, in a spacious house in a tree-lined neighborhood, three children were born: Yoka in 1934, Francisca in 1937, and Otto in 1939. Life was comfortable, similar to that of other young Dutch upper middle-class families. But that life came to an abrupt end in May 1940, when the Germans overran the Netherlands in five days.

Mindful of Holland's long-standing tradition of tolerance, the Germans took their time in launching their campaign whose ultimate goal, in Holland as elsewhere, was to kill every single Jew they could lay their hands on. In the first year Jews were dismissed from the Dutch press, forbidden to practice ritual slaughter, and barred from joining their Dutch neighbors in civil defense maneuvers—a modest beginning but a beginning none the less. But early in 1941 the Germans stepped up the pace of persecution. Jews were thrown out of their jobs and gradually ghettoized. In May 1942, they were forced to wear the yellow star (which they had to display even in Westerbork), and three months later they were being "resettled" for "labor service" in the East by the thousands.

Nazi decrees aimed specifically at Jews forced Gerrit out of his business and Yoka, then eight years old, out of her second-grade class. When the Nazis commandeered their home, the Verdoners went to live with Gerrit's parents in Amsterdam. Shortly thereafter, seeing the writing on the wall, Gerrit and Hilde decided to place the children in hiding, and with the help of the underground found suitable homes for them. Their foresight enabled the children to survive, and thus to prepare these letters for publication.

Hilde entered Westerbork on December 18, 1942, and, except for two periods when she was briefly released, stayed there for more than a year—far longer than most Jews managed to hang on. The reason for the breaks in her captivity, in June and September 1943, and the lengthy sojourn in Westerbork, was that her husband, Gerrit, had a job with the Jewish Council, the body established by the Germans to serve as a conduit between the hunter and the hunted. Employees of the Jewish Council were the beneficiaries of the most sought-after commodity in the Jewish world, exemption from deportation. Gerrit's job as a courier and a buyer of supplies for Westerbork gave him the freedom to travel about relatively unimpeded and accounts for his ability to fulfill Hilde's many requests for food and assorted personal articles (combs, toothbrushes, toilet paper), items that enabled his wife to bear up under Westerbork's regime rather better than the average inmate. But after the Jewish Council had virtually administered itself out of existence, and the bulk of the Jews had been funneled to the East in the course of 1943, the exemptions came to nought as well. Gerrit himself disappeared and went into hiding.

Unlike Hilde, most Jews were dispatched speedily, sometimes only hours after they arrived at the camp. But whether the Jews who entered Westerbork stayed hours, days, weeks, months, or longer, a single passion consumed them all: to remain in the camp as long as possible, for they sensed that Poland meant their extinction. Accordingly, they strained every muscle and exhausted every possible means to stay clear of the trains. Some Jews purchased their "freedom from transport," paying exorbitant amounts of money for a place on a so-called exemption list. Others tried to prove that Aryan blood coursed through their veins; others again professed to be Protestants or Catholics. Sephardic Jews claimed to be citizens of Portugal, and quite a few inmates carried passports proclaiming them to be citizens of Holland as well as some South or Central American country. They had purchased the passports when that was still feasible. Many strove to acquire jobs in Westerbork that the Germans considered vital to the war effort such as shoemaking, clothing manufacturing, metal sorting. Westerbork had "Cultural Jews" (Jews exempted from deportation by virtue of their importance to Holland's cultural and educational life, a concession wrung from the German rulers by a couple of influential Dutch officials) and "Palestine Jews" (holders of certificates granting entry into British-controlled Palestine) and a host of other categories which permitted their recipients to linger on in the camp "until further notice." Some of the lists were "better" than others, but none was foolproof—a situation that prompted Philip Mechanicus, a journalist who kept a diary in Westerbork, to define an exemption list as "a collection of Jews who will one day be deported."

Westerbork was built by the Dutch government to house refugees from Hitler's Germany who had illegally crossed the border into the Netherlands, and the first Jews arrived there in the fall of 1939. Situated on a barren patch of heath in Drente, a province in Holland's east, Westerbork was an inhospitable place—hot and dusty in summer; cold, wet, and muddy in winter; plagued by sand, storm, and flies. Large barracks, erected within a space of half-a-square kilometer, dominated the skyline, interspersed with some 200 "little houses" built along the same lines as the barracks and connected under one roof. The barracks were oblong shelters, about 50 meters in length, ten meters wide, and five-to-six meters high, with a latrine for each of the sexes. Each barrack was designed to accommodate up to 300 people, but they often held twice as many. The "little houses" consisted of two or three small rooms, a toilet, and an electric hotplate. Though not inconsiderable, the compound was hardly equipped to cope with the flow of "transport material" that came streaming through the gate in the years 1942 and 1943.

Even so, and aside from the weekly (and sometimes twice-weekly) transports, life in Westerbork was not unbearable, at least not when measured against conditions that we know prevailed in other camps. There were many rules but none that could not be bent with a little ingenuity. Discipline was lax. Hilde wrote and received many letters outside the official channels, and routinely smuggled food to friends held in the camp's prison. Inmates did not work themselves to death; on the contrary, their lack of zeal was a constant source of concern for the heads of the workshops who could be deported for not meeting their production quotas. The fare was mostly adequate, if lackluster—Hilde refers to it as "the ubiquitous mush"—hence her many food requests. No one walked in fear of being suddenly struck down by a bullet or club. Yet, prisoners did well to mind their p's and q's. "Here we were not being kicked or beaten," stated a former inmate of Westerbork at the postwar trial of the camp's German commandant, "but the punishment was much subtler. Because for every mild transgression you were sent on transport, and that meant death."

As long as the transports ran smoothly Westerbork's commandant, Albert Konrad Gemmeker, preferred to let the Jews take care of things, placing them in charge of every facet of the camp. Jews ran the hospital, the first aid station, the school and the nursery. They staffed the camp police and fire brigade; they handled the laundry and operated the central kitchen and bathhouse; they took care of the maintenance and ran the workshops; they put on cabarets and musical programs; they organized boxing and soccer matches; they helped people prepare for the transports. Westerbork had Jewish barbers, Jewish hair dressers, Jewish doctors and dentists, Jewish policemen and Jewish firemen. There was a "store" for Jews and a café for Jews. Such was the insanity of a system that "pampered" its victims before bundling them off to be killed further down the road.

Even though the Germans extolled Westerbork as a "model camp," its atmosphere was thick with tension. The grating of tempers stretched by the will to live produced that "war of nerves" which was the hallmark of life in Westerbork. Apart form the ever-present fear of the transports, the tension was further exacerbated by the diversity of the inmates. Westerbork's Dutch and German Jews accounted for the majority, but there were also colonies of Czech, Polish, Rumanian, Hungarian, Russian, Turkish, Spanish, and Italian Jews. There were gypsies as well as Jewish converts to Christianity, nuns and priests. Every shade of religious opinion and observance could be found there, as could every social class and form of political expression. (Like most Dutch Jews, Hilde seems to have been indifferent to religion.) There were children (who stayed with their mothers on the female side of the large barracks), adolescents, and people in the twilight of life.

All of these were lumped together in barracks that never seemed big enough to hold them all. Hilde complains constantly both of the lack of space for her belongings and the lack of privacy for herself, the battles around the stoves, the inadequacy of the toilet facilities, and so on. Not surprisingly, squabbles were the order of the day. Hilde, however, seems to have had a flexible and sharing nature and the capacity to take things in stride. Her personal prescription for coping: Prepare for the worst and then decide to make the best of it.

As in every society, even a society that lived with its ears cocked to the sound of the trains, Westerbork had its own pecking order. Apart from the German Commandant, who ruled supreme, the top of the pyramid belonged to the Jews who had been in the camp the longest and who spoke the same language as the occupier. These were the German Jews, the most envied and the most despised of the camp population. The envy derived from the fact that their camp cards were stamped with the letters "ST" (short for *Stamlijst* or Basic List) which gave them the best protection from deportation Westerbork had to offer, for the Basic List was the Commandant's personal exemption list. The loathing was fueled by the high-handed manner in which the German Jews wielded their power, as most of them held the top posts in Westerbork's extensive administrative apparatus. Led by Kurt Schlesinger, dubbed the "Jewish Commandant" by his enemies, the Long-Term Residents, as they were officially known, ate, lived, and dressed better than the run-of-the-mill inmate and were among the last to be deported. Most of them ended up, not in Auschwitz, the destination of Westerbork's unprotected masses, but in Theresienstadt, the "picturesque little fortress town" in Bohemia touted by the Germans as a "Model Ghetto."

One of the principal functions of the Jewish "aristocracy" was to prepare the deportation lists. The quota of Jews to be deported each week was set by the German Security Police in the Hague and telexed to Commandant Gemmeker in Westerbork, who would then pass the information on to his Jewish administrators with instructions to draw up the list from Westerbork's available "transport material." Who was to be selected for "labor service in the East" was left largely to the discretion of the top-level Jewish administrators. The main thing was that the required number of Jews boarded the trains.

As every Jew sought to save his own skin, it stands to reason that in their composition of the transports the Jewish elite would in the first instance strive to protect their friends and relatives, as well as anyone else blessed with their favor. This led to a great deal of bitterness, especially among the Dutch Jews who made up the camp's majority and who felt, not without reason, that they were getting the short end of the stick. But there is no reason to assume that they would have acted differently had the roles been reversed.

None of this resentment is reflected in Hilde's letters. She seems to have been on good terms with Westerbork's luminaries. Owing to her secretarial job in one of Westerbork's busier administrative offices, she must have rubbed shoulders with them daily. For example, in her letters she occasionally refers to "Schles." or simply "S", and from the context the reference could only be to Kurt Schlesinger, whose official title was Camp Elder. She also alludes to visits she made to the "little houses," the preferred housing enjoyed by the camp's Jewish aristocracy. She writes to Gerrit in March of 1943:

> It was an unusual sensation once again to sit around a table under a lamp with a small group of people, to be drinking tea (sorry, it was coffee) from a regular cup, and without seeing a crowd of people shuffling by all the time; and to be able to keep up a conversation without being interrupted, without having to get up all the time to let someone pass to climb into his bed which just happens to be behind the bench you're sitting on.

All indications are that Hilde was well supplied with "Vitamin C," as Westerbork's inmates half-jokingly referred to the benefits to be derived from knowing the right people, the "C" standing for Connections.

But when the final curtain was about to come down, Hilde's connections were evidently not enough to keep her name off the transport list. Her "fall from grace" was probably triggered by the collapse of the Jewish Council and Gerrit's narrow escape from the clutches of the Germans; he happened to be away on September 29, 1943, the day on which the Germans scooped up the last Jews from the streets of Amsterdam and conveyed them to the transit camp. The seized included Hilde, who had been released from Westerbork only ten days earlier. It was a blow from which she never recovered.

When she returned to the camp following this final roundup, Hilde no longer had the secretarial job which in the past had provided some measure of protection. The loss of this job, combined with the collapse of Gerrit's exemption and his subsequent disappearance, placed Hilde in immediate danger of deportation, and from then on she had to find and fight her own way to an exemption. At the same time, she worried about the future of her own parents and the parents of her husband, both sets of parents being in Westerbork. The parents were presumed safe because they were on the "120." Jews who held stamps in this "120,000 series"—primarily Jews with influence and contacts in enemy states—were to be kept back for possible exchange against German nationals in Allied hands. As was often the case with exemptions, this stamp could also be bought.

For herself, Hilde considered several options. One of these was the so-called Calmeyer List. Calmeyer was a lawyer in the German Department of Justice whose job it was to examine the blood credentials of Jews claiming to be Aryans. To qualify, the prospective Aryan was required to submit proof of Aryan ancestry on one side and could not be married to a Jew or have been a member of the Jewish community before May 10, 1940, the day of the German invasion. To this end, Hilde writes Gerrit to suggest that he find someone to testify that a deceased non-Jewish uncle of his "was your father."

Hilde also briefly toyed with securing a place on the "Weinreb List." Friedrich Weinreb, an orthodox Jew, claimed that he had a list, approved by the German High Command, which would enable those on it to emigrate to South America in exchange for foreign funds and German prisoners. But the list, which operated even in Westerbork, turned out to be a fraud. After the war Weinreb, its sponsor, was found guilty of collaboration and spent a number of years in a Dutch prison.

Finally, she tried to protect herself by finding employment that offered a better chance of staying on in Westerbork than the childcare she was doing after she had been reinserted into the ranks of the inmates at the end of September. "I may try to be assigned to the sewing workshop," she informed her husband in November 1943.

There was one other course open to Hilde: escape. Escape was not difficult, but not many Jews tried it. The principal reason was that escapes were punished by reprisals directed not only at the fugitive's kin but also at his barrack mates, who would find themselves on the next train to Auschwitz. From his hideout on a farm in Friesland, the neighboring province, Gerrit again and again urged his wife to escape, informing her by means of coded messages of the steps he was taking or could take to make it happen. He even sent people from the underground into the camp to pull her out. " . . . but she always said," wrote Gerrit in a postwar letter, "that she wanted to wait a little longer." Hilde would not escape because she could not bring herself to accept the "decidedly immoral aspect of it." Only after other family members had left, Hilde assures her husband, would she attempt an escape.

But it never came to that. Some time early in December Hilde fell ill with hepatitis, and all of her last letters were written from a hospital bed. As the camp became emptier and emptier and friends and relatives continued to vanish in an easterly direction, one after the other, she found it harder and harder to keep up her morale. Her brother Otto left on the transport of January 11, 1944, to Zelle (Bergen Belsen, the "exchange camp" near Hanover). The same train also unexpectedly swallowed her beloved Aunt Selma and Uncle Paul. Hilde's strength ebbed away and with it the optimism that in the past had helped her to sustain the belief that somehow things would turn out all right. Feeling powerless, she continued to worry about the parents who were not "resourceful enough" to scrounge for bread, and in her last letter from Westerbork, dated January 31, 1944, she expressed her anxiety over the status of the various family members still left in Westerbork. And to Gerrit she wrote: "Take care and keep your spirits up." Her last words to him.

When twenty-four hours before her deportation Hilde launched her desperate "Do what you can!" appeal to her father, she was clearly asking him to pull whatever strings he could to get her name removed from the deportation scroll. But evidently no one was in a position to help. As he went about his rounds in a fruitless quest to save his daughter, Hilde's father no doubt heard what countless inmates had heard before him: "There is nothing to be done."

The trains had to be filled—always—even if in this instance it meant emptying hospital beds and disbanding the orphanage. And in the small hours of the morning of the eighth, a wet and miserable day, Hilde was forced from her hospital bed and delivered to the cattle train in an open cart. Not long thereafter, the train set off in an easterly direction.

Westerbork was liberated in April 1945. Of the Verdoners and Sluizers who were in the camp, only Hilde's parents managed to survive, via Theresienstadt.

The reader who expects Hilde's letters to be filled with philosophical reflections and "deep thought" will come away disappointed. Hilde Verdoner-Sluizer was no Etty Hillesum or Philip Mechanicus, inmates of Westerbork whose writings about the camp have been internationally acclaimed. Etty Hillesum, a young woman intent on becoming a writer, considered it her duty "to bear witness," to be "the eyes and ears of a fragment of Jewish history." Philip Mechanicus was a journalist to whom writing was as natural as eating and breathing. Hilde, by contrast, did not write for posterity or the general public. Her letters were addressed to her husband, parents, and friends, and are filled with the kind of private matters one would expect from a devoted mother, wife, and daughter. But she was certainly literate, and in reading her letters we get to hear not just Hilde's voice but the voice of the average Jew. For in the final analysis the story of the Holocaust is the story of millions of Jews like Hilde, people who are seldom heard from—hence the value of *Signs of Life*. To read it is to experience the Holocaust at ground level.

Jacob Boas
Holocaust Center of Northern California

Time Line

April 20, 1889—Adolf Hitler is born in the Austrian town of Braunau.

1918—Hitler declares that he feels called upon by Providence to devote his life to the struggle against the Jews.

1919—Hitler joins the Deutsche Arbeiterpartei (German Workers' Party), a small, nationalistic, anti-Semitic political circle. The same year, he declares, somewhat vaguely, that the ultimate objective of his anti-Semitism is "the removal of Jews altogether."

1920—Hitler establishes himself as Führer (leader) of the party, which has in the meantime become the National-Sozialistische Deutsche Arbeiterpartei (NSDAP, or Nazis).

1923—While serving part of a jail sentence for an attempted overthrow of the German government, Hitler writes volume 1 of his autobiography, *Mein Kampf* ("My Struggle"), in which he declares that between twelve thousand and fifteen thousand Jews should have been gassed in World War I. Volume 2 is published in 1927.

January 30, 1933—President Hindenburg appoints Adolf Hitler as Reich Chancellor (Prime Minister) of Germany.

March 10, 1933—First concentration camp, Dachau, is established on the site of a former gunpowder factory eleven miles northwest of Munich.

March 21, 1933—In Amsterdam, Abraham Asscher and David Cohen establish the Comité voor Bijzondere Joodse Belangen ("Committee for Special Jewish Affairs") to aid German-Jewish refugees, who are fleeing to the Netherlands in ever-increasing numbers. Asscher is president of the Dutch-Jewish communities, and Cohen, a long-time, active Zionist and professor of ancient history. The committee's prime task is to assist refugees and facilitate their further emigration. It also engages in some anti-Nazi propaganda.

April 1, 1933—Nazis proclaim a general boycott of all Jewish-owned businesses in Germany.

April 7, 1933—German Jews are dismissed from civil service and denied admission to the bar.

April 26—Formation of the Gestapo.

May 10, 1933—Burning of books by Jews and opponents of Nazism.

December 1, 1933—Hitler declares legal unity of the German State and the Nazi Party.

August 2, 1934—Hindenburg dies. Hitler becomes head of state and commander in chief of the armed forces.

September 15, 1935—The Nuremberg Laws create a legal definition of "Jew," and establish a clear distinction between German and Jewish "blood." The "Law for the Protection of German Blood and Honor" forbids any union, marital or other, between these two categories. All subsequent anti-Jewish decrees of the Third Reich emanate from definitions set by the Nuremberg Laws. The Nuremberg Laws also strip German Jews of their citizenship.

July 16, 1937—Buchenwald concentration camp opens.

March 13, 1938—Austria is annexed to the Third Reich. Nazis apply anti-Semitic laws.

July 6, 1938—At an international conference in Evian, France, the United States expresses concern for the plight of German Jews, but no action is taken.

October 5, 1938—Passports of Jews are marked with the letter "J."

November 9 and 10, 1938—Perhaps the most famous German *Aktion*, or anti-Jewish raid, Kristallnacht ("Night of Broken Glass") is unleashed by the Nazis. Anti-Semitic riots spread throughout Germany and Austria. In what the German government later attempts to portray as a spontaneous outburst on the part of the "Aryan" population, 815 Jewish shops are destroyed; 29 warehouses and 171 dwellings are set on fire or otherwise destroyed; 191 synagogues are set on fire, and 76 more are demolished. Thirty-six Jews are killed, and another 36 are severely injured. None of the subsequent Jewish insurance claims are honored. After the riots, the German government imposes a fine of one billion marks on the Jewish population, ostensibly to pay for the damage; in reality, however, the fine helps to finance Germany's rearmament.

Signs of Life

Following Kristallnacht, emigration from Germany increases.

November 15, 1938—Jewish children are expelled from German schools.

January, 1939—By this time, the Committee for Special Jewish Affairs has spent some three million Dutch guilders ($780,000) in aiding German Jewish refugees. The funds come mainly from the Jewish community in the Netherlands.

January 30, 1939—Hitler "prophesies" that a new world war will lead to the extermination of the Jewish race in Europe.

1939—The Netherlands is now host to approximately thirty thousand German Jewish refugees. Except for the leaders, the Committee for Special Jewish Affairs comprises almost exclusively German Jews. Because of the increase in anti-Jewish measures in Germany, the committee's expenses have risen to three million guilders yearly. The Dutch government, which has resisted a more liberal immigration policy, establishes a central camp for illegal aliens at Westerbork, near the German border.

February, 1939—The financial burden of Westerbork falls on the committee: it is taxed two hundred thousand guilders annually, effective immediately.

March 15, 1939—Germany occupies Czechoslovakia.

September 1, 1939—German Army invades Poland. World War II begins.

September 3, 1939—Britain and France declare war on Germany.

October 9, 1939—The first group of German-Jewish refugees arrives at Westerbork.

October 12, 1939—The first deportation of Jews from Austria and Moravia leaves for Poland.

November 23, 1939—Wearing of the Judenstern (Jewish, six-pointed Star of David) is made compulsory throughout occupied Poland.

April 9, 1940—Germany invades Denmark and Norway.

April 27, 1940—Himmler establishes Auschwitz death camp in Poland.

May 10, 1940—Germany invades Holland, Belgium, and France.

May 14, 1940—The Dutch capitulate to German forces. The royal family and cabinet having fled to England, the Netherlands is left without a government, at the mercy of the Nazis.

June 22, 1940—France surrenders to the Germans.

September, 1940—Jews in the Netherlands are barred from certain residential districts and some professions, including all public service. All civil servants are forced to sign declarations stating they are "Aryan." All Jewish newspapers are banned by German authorities.

November 18, 1940—All Jewish civil servants and teachers in Holland are dismissed.

January 24, 1941—The Germans mandate registration and special identity cards for all Jews. The same month, the Dutch Ashkenazi and Sephardic communities, in cooperation with national Jewish communities, respond by instituting the Committee of Coordination, which seeks to form a unified stand in the Jewish population. The committee's president, Lodewyk E. Visser, categorically refuses to cooperate with any anti-Jewish measure. Asscher and Cohen disagree, hoping to alleviate suffering by cooperation with the Germans.

February 12, 1941—In response to violence which has arisen between Jews and Dutch Nazis, the Jewish quarter of Amsterdam is sealed off at 6:00 A.M. The same day, the Jewish Council is established by German order, to serve as a liaison between Germans and Jews. Asscher and Cohen are its presidents. The apparatus of the Committee for Special Jewish Affairs is incorporated into the Jewish Council, which increasingly supplants the Committee of Coordination. The first task of the newly formed council is to call upon all Jews to surrender their weapons. Evidence strongly suggests that the Jews of Amsterdam had no weapons in the first place; thus, very few are relinquished to the Nazis.

February 22 and 23, 1941—In response to a German officer's being sprayed with ammonia at a Jewish ice-cream parlor two days earlier, the Germans descend on the Jews *en masse*. Four hundred Jewish men between the ages of twenty and thirty-five are arrested and sent to Buchenwald, and then to Mauthausen.

February 25 and 26, 1941—The Communist Party in Amsterdam organizes a strike to protest the deportation. Dutch Jews and Gentiles alike stand together against the Nazis. The strike is widely observed, and is the only one of its kind throughout Europe for the duration of the war. In response, the Germans threaten to shoot five hundred Jews. At Asscher's request, the strike ceases.

April 11, 1941—First appearance of *Het Joodsche Weekblad,* the German-controlled, Jewish weekly which is now the only legal Jewish publication in the Netherlands. Although at first it publishes cultural articles, and attempts to boost the morale of the Jewish population, it soon becomes a mere vehicle for announcements of the Jewish Council.

May 11, 1941—*Einsatzgruppen* are given an oral directive to kill all Jews. These "special task forces" are mobile S.S. units assigned to combat the civilian enemy by various methods, including mass murder.

June 22, 1941—Germany attacks the Soviet Union.

July 8, 1941—Wearing of the Jewish star is decreed in the German-occupied Baltic states.

July 31, 1941—In a letter, Hermann Goering gives Reinhard Heydrich, head of the Reich Security Main Office, the order to "proceed with all the preparations necessary for organizing the complete solution of the Jewish question in the German sphere of influence in Europe."

August, 1941—In a measure intended by the Germans to isolate the Dutch Jewish population further, Jewish children are removed from public schools in The Netherlands. An extensive system of Jewish schools is established and supervised by the Jewish Council.

All Jewish property is transferred to the bank of Lippmann, Rosenthal, and Company, which had originally been a Jewish bank. In this way, a total of three hundred million to four hundred million guilders ($1 million) is extracted from the Dutch Jews. Twenty percent is used for financing the Jewish Council, the camps at Vught and Westerbork, and the Jews involved. The rest is transferred to German institutions.

September 15, 1941—The wearing of the Jewish star is decreed throughout the Greater Reich.

September 23, 1941—At Auschwitz, the Nazis conduct the first experiments with gassing.

October 27, 1941—The Germans extend the power of the Jewish Council over all of Holland, and order the Committee of Coordination to suspend its activities. Representatives responsible to the Jewish Council are appointed in each province and in Rotterdam.

    At its climax, the Jewish Council has perhaps seventeen thousand members. It is now the only legal Jewish voice in the Netherlands, for the Germans have banned all previously existing Jewish groups, and confiscated their funds. Any such groups have now been incorporated into the Jewish Council.

December 8, 1941—The United States enters the war. The same day, the Chelmno extermination camp on the Ner River in Poland opens.

January 20, 1942—Following Goering's letter of July 31, 1941, Heydrich convenes a conference of top Nazi officials at the central office of Interpol in Wannsee, a suburb of Berlin. Hitler himself is not present. The goal of the Wannsee Conference is to streamline the operation of liquidating European Jewry, including those in Britain, which the Germans hope to conquer in due course. Heydrich announces that "the Final Solution of the Jewish Question in Europe should be applied to about eleven million persons."

1942—By early 1942, over 50 percent of Holland's Jews are concentrated in the three ghetto sections of Amsterdam. The same year, the Jewish Council co-operates with the Germans in establishing forty-two labor camps all over Holland. Over five thousand men from eighty-five towns and cities in

Holland are incarcerated in the prison system to work on development projects, some of which are entirely superfluous. The inmates, all male, endure inhuman conditions: in one typical camp, they are allowed 2.8 ounces of butter per week, plus seven ounces of bread and a single (mostly liquid) ladle of warm food daily. This is their fare for nine-and-a-half hour workdays of hard labor.

May 9, 1942—The Nazis decree that all Dutch Jews are to wear the yellow star, which is intended to isolate and degrade them in the eyes of their fellow citizens. The Jewish Council is compelled to cooperate with the implementation of the order. The Dutch population, including some individuals in National Socialist (Nazi) circles, resists the order, and in protest, non-Jews distribute and wear the star-shaped badge themselves. The Germans report that the Jews wear their stars proudly, but are frightened by the new, anti-Jewish measures. Ultimately, of course, the wearing of the stars paves the way for mass deportations.

June 1, 1942—Treblinka death camp opens in Poland.

Summer 1942 through September 1944—Mass deportations of Jews from the Netherlands are initiated and completed by the Germans. The Germans call the operation "Arbeitseinsatz im Osten" ("Work in the East") in order to disguise its true nature. In reality, deportation means death in the extermination camps, in particular Auschwitz.

Initially, the Germans try calling up young people by mail. When only a few present themselves, arrests follow.

July 1, 1942—The Germans take command of Westerbork, after expanding it considerably.

July 16, 1942—Westerbork is proclaimed a *Polizeiliches Durchgangslager* ("Police-Transit Camp"). Those inmates who have arrived as German-Jewish refugees are made responsible for the internal management and organization of the camp, including arranging transports to the east. Of those who are so transported, the majority are sent to Auschwitz, which ultimately consumes sixty thousand people from Westerbork. Thirty-four thousand are sent to Sobibor, where they are gassed upon arrival. Five thousand former Westerbork inmates, mostly prominent personalities, are sent to Theresienstadt, and four thousand are sent to Bergen-Belsen. This last group is intended for exchange with other countries, and indeed, 75 percent do survive the war. Some are exchanged for Germans in other lands, 136 eventually arrive in Switzerland, and 222 manage to reach Palestine.

October 2, 1942—A large-scale German *Aktion* (raid) is conducted throughout Holland, in all suitable locations. Whole families, including 8,877 women and children, are arrested. As a result of this single *Aktion*, thirteen thousand Jews are imprisoned in Westerbork, then sent to Auschwitz.

April 19, 1943 to May 16, 1943—The Jews in the Warsaw Ghetto stage an uprising. Armed only with two machine guns, light artillery, Molotov cocktails, and rocks, they manage to keep the well-equipped and highly trained German army at bay for four months. Ultimately, however, the Warsaw Ghetto is liquidated.

February 24, 1943—Hitler states, "This struggle will not end with the annihilation of Aryan mankind, but with the extermination of the Jewish people in Europe."

April 13, 1943—With very few exceptions, all Dutch Jews are legally required to live in Amsterdam. The new ruling is part of the German effort to make Holland "Judenrein" ("clean of Jews").

August 2, 1943—Prisoners at Treblinka revolt. Between 150 and 200 of the 700 inmates escape; all are recaptured.

business in Amsterdam. The business was located in the basement of the seventeenth-century house on the Prins Hendrikkade, where Gerrit grew up. Ultimately, this business grew into the Magneet Bicycle Factory in Weesp, managed by Gerrit at the time of his marriage to Hilde.

Gerrit had two older sisters, Caroline and Suze, and one younger sister, Josephine. Our aunts survived the war. We remember very little of our Verdoner grandparents, however, as they too were killed by the Nazis.

❧ ❧ ❧

The stories told to us about our mother reveal her to have been an independent and self-confident individual. Our grandfather told us how his daughter defied his authority while she was away in Italy where she had gone to study and work. Ordered to come home, she flatly refused. When he threatened to cut off her allowance if she didn't heed his summons, she replied that she hoped he would not be angry but that she was well able to support herself on what she was earning and that she wasn't quite ready to return to Holland yet.

The Nazis too got a taste of Hilde's defiance. In the spring of 1942, the local German commandant selected our street in Hilversum as an attractive location to billet his officers, forcing us out of our home. In spite of her lack of interest in housekeeping or gardening, Hilde had nevertheless planted bulbs in our garden for the first time that year, and now those flowers would be there for the Nazis to enjoy. Hilde was enraged. One spring day, when the tulips were in full bloom and the Germans were away at their offices, she returned to our front yard in broad daylight and carried the flowers off by the armful. It was a typical gesture for Hilde and a small way of protesting the loss of our home, our family life, our entire existence.

In reading the letters Hilde wrote from Westerbork we seem to hear echoes of this independent spirit. We hear them as she repeatedly turns down Gerrit's pleas to her to escape. We hear them as she expresses her conviction that she can take care of herself even under difficult circumstances. We hear them as she tries to cheer herself up by imagining the barracks in Westerbork to be not unlike the lodgings of a Swiss chalet on a ski trip. She had never yet come up against a situation she could not handle with ease, and it did not become clear to her until the final months before she died that these were not ordinary circumstances that would yield to her energy and resilience.

Our mother made the choice not to escape from Westerbork because it would have meant the immediate deportation of her parents, her brother Otto, and her parents-in-law. She did not wish to escape at the cost of their lives. Thus she became one of the six million Jewish victims of the Nazi era.

We wish we could have known her.

🌿 🌿 🌿

Instead of growing up with our mother and father in a home of our own, we spent most of the war years with other families. It is to this we owe our survival—three among the small number of Dutch Jewish children who were still alive after the war. In the summer of 1942, realizing that it was no longer safe to keep us with them, our parents had the foresight and the courage to give us up in order to place us with other people. With the help of the underground, they found three hiding places.

Yoka initially spent some months in a children's home, but when the underground got word that the home was about to be raided by the Nazis, she was spirited away. She subsequently spent a few weeks with Grada and Hans van de Beek, our former Nanny and her husband, recently married and expecting their first child. Finally, from January 1943 until the end of the war, Yoka lived with Dick and Ella Rijnders in the village of Woubrugge, situated in typical Dutch farm country.

Dick Rijnders was the mayor of this village, among

the last ones to be appointed by the legitimate Dutch government. Throughout the war the Germans remained unaware of Dick's ties to the underground. The reason given to friends and neighbors for Yoka's stay in Woubrugge was that her mother was ill in a sanatorium in Switzerland. To the inhabitants of the village Yoka was known as "Yoka van de burgemeester," the "mayor's Yoka." Though just eight years old, Yoka understood the situation completely; she never made a mistake about her real last name or the reason she was living with the Rijnders. When she visited the village as an adult many years later, the farmers still recognized her and greeted her like an old neighbor.

Unlike Yoka, Fran, at the age of five, was too young to comprehend what was happening. Separation from her parents, living with strangers and having to call them Mama and Papa for the sake of safety, caused much confusion and difficulty. Jan and Fen Barens lived in the lovely seacoast resort town of Zandvoort when Fran came to live with them in the fall of 1942. Shortly afterwards, however, they were forced from their home when the Germans fortified the town in anticipation of an allied invasion. The Barens, with Fran, moved to a Jewish neighborhood in Amsterdam where many houses had become available because the rightful owners had been recently deported. It is clear from Hilde's letters, in which the name Jan Barens is frequently mentioned, that he was active in the resistance movement and did much to help the Jews and others persecuted by the Nazis.

Otto spent the war years in the farming hamlet of Diepenveen, near Arnhem. There he was taken in by Wiete and Maria Hopperus Buma. Both Wiete and Maria had been widowed when they met and their marriage created a large blended family with his three and her two teen-age children. By the time they took Otto in, their own children ranged in age from twelve to twenty-two, all living in a large villa aptly called "Huize Refugium" or "House of Refuge." Not only Otto, but others too were hidden there from the Germans from time to time. Otto has few memories of those years,

Signs of Life

37

except for having to go upstairs when strangers approached the house and seeing the dog fights over Arnhem during the Battle of Arnhem in 1944. One day after Diepenveen had been liberated, another stranger approached the house. Otto opened the door and ran to tell Maria that there was a bald man at the door with a car, a rarity in those days. The "stranger" turned out to be Otto's father, who had finally come to get him.

We owe a debt of gratitude to the "aunts" and "uncles" who selflessly took us in at great risk to themselves. They could so easily have looked the other way but instead they chose to save us.

As for our mother, only her letters survive.

🌿 🌿 🌿

As we tell elsewhere, our father, who like us survived the war in hiding, died of cancer in October 1947. After his death, we children passed the letters from one to the other, but not until almost forty years later did we muster the courage to look at them closely. We realized that their existence placed an obligation on us to preserve them in a more permanent form. That is the reason for this book which we hope will enable us, Hilde's children, as well as her grandchildren and future generations, to know something about our mother and the terrible events that overtook her.

The first two letters and the extract from a third were written by Gerrit at the end of the war to two of his sisters. They describe in chronological order and detail the events of those years as well as some of Gerrit's own experiences in hiding. These are followed by two letters written by Hilde in 1942, before the family separated. All the subsequent letters were written from Westerbork. No changes have been made in Hilde's letters. Nothing has been omitted.

Yoka Verdoner
Francisca Verdoner Kan
1989

Hilde Verdoner-Sluizer, 1942.

The Lost Pearl

for Hilde Verdoner-Sluizer
(1909-1944)

Click and caught,
framed and fit in glass,
wearing black with white lace
forever knotted around your neck;
your skin is satin smooth
not grandmotherly
as I want it to be.

Looking at me with mother-eyes,
your right eye dares me
to climb alps and swim channels.
Your other dares me to write.
I try to read your life
in eyes that watch me water
plants, sit at my desk, lie
in bed reading, sleeping, making love.
These eyes stare at me in my mirror.

In rooms spread across this country,
doubles and triples of you watch
my sisters and cousins, aunt, uncle, and mother.

We hold each other, silently
confirming our life and wondering who
you might have been.
I wear a ring you weren't wearing
the day they took you away.
Its three pearls come unglued and get lost
one at a time, and over and over
like a mesmerized child
I replace them as though resetting
a pearl beside the others
keeps our lives together.

With the tattered thin letters
you wrote to arbitrary survivors,
we invent a script for you: plans
for your children, for yourself,
family secrets, recipes for cooking,
recipes for living. But your mid-sentence
stories were stolen from your broad forehead
like wedding rings off fingers,
like pendants half-hidden
at the V at your neck,
like children.

I keep looking to see
if you are afraid. I want
to set you in my mind as surely
as I set this photograph on my shelf.
Heir of the ache in my mother's eyes,
I cry for your songs, the ones
you hummed as you combed your hair
to a clip at the back of your head.

Susan Kan
1988

Signs of Life

Family home in Hilversum.

Gerrit and Hilde's wedding on December 12, 1933. Left to right: Jettie Fontijn, Lettie Stibbe, Miep Sluizer, Fannie Schönberg, Hilde, Gerrit, Bertha Sluizer, David Sluizer, Henriette Verdoner, Abraham Verdoner.

Signs of Life

43

GERRIT'S LETTERS
TO HIS SISTERS
1945

Gerrit Verdoner, 1945.

Introduction
To Gerrit's Letters

The first letters in this book were written by Gerrit to his sisters in the United States and Belgium. Caroline (or Lien), the oldest, had left just before the war with her husband Ben and their daughter Lettie. She lived in New York. Jo, with her husband Barend and two teenage sons, had escaped in 1942. Their perilous journey across the borders of Belgium, France, and Spain, and then across the Atlantic Ocean, is a story in itself. At the end of the war, Jo and Barend were also living in New York. Suze, Gerrit's third sister, had been safe because she was married to a Catholic, René. They lived in Antwerp with two of their daughters.

Aside from a telegram informing them that Gerrit and the three children were alive, the letters in this section were the first detailed account relatives in America received after the war, telling them about the terrible events that had taken place during the intervening years—the deaths of their parents and Hilde and of many other relatives and friends who had disappeared in, as Gerrit put it, "a deliberate, carefully planned system of annihilation."

We have placed Gerrit's letters first because they pro-vide an overview of the events that took place during the war and thus make it easier to understand Hilde's letters, which form the main body of this book. The letters also reveal Ger-rit's own feelings about the tumultuous events he had lived through, his joy at finding his children alive, his anger and sadness at the deaths of his wife and parents, and his tortured feelings that he should have done more to save them. Gerrit blames himself especially for not having saved his father and mother.

At the time Gerrit had to decide how best to protect his parents, Abraham and Henriette Verdoner, they were both well over seventy. Gerrit believed, as did many others in his position, that his job with the Jewish Council would pro-tect his parents and give them a better chance to survive than going into hiding. Going into hiding in their case would have meant remaining indoors, literally hidden, for months or years, dependent on others for shelter, food, and safety, in constant danger of betrayal. Gerrit believed that they would be unable to deal with the stresses of such a situation and, like many others in similar circumstances, would be caught. The letters reveal his sense of failure and guilt that he had been unable to save them—a feeling which many survivors consciously or unconsciously experienced. Even children who survived the war as we did came away with this legacy of the Nazi era, the feeling that they should have been able to save their parents or have died with them.

A few words of explanation regarding the role of the Jewish Council are perhaps in order here. Whenever the Ger-mans invaded a country, they had the Jewish community in that country organize a leadership council. The nature of this council was ambiguous. Some Jews believed that the ex-istence of the Jewish Council gave them a measure of control over their own fate. In reality, however, the Germans used these councils to enable the organization of arrests and de-portations to proceed more smoothly. Gerrit refers to the raid of September 29, 1943, in which Hilde, his parents, and

Signs of Life

his in-laws were arrested. This was the final big raid in Amsterdam during which the Germans also arrested the "entire Jewish Council, including Ascher and Cohen." Abraham Ascher and Professor David Cohen were the controversial joint chairmen of the Jewish Council in The Netherlands; they carried out German directives in order, so they said, to "prevent worse things from happening." Gerrit's job with the Jewish Council was to buy food supplies for the camps. This enabled him to go to Westerbork regularly and see Hilde. He was also able to leave the camp again, at least for a time, and ironically his absence supposedly protected Hilde from deportation.

Gerrit's letters also give a clear picture of his own experiences during the time he went into hiding and afterwards. His descriptions of life on the farm in Drente are vivid and hilarious. Gerrit's joy at being reunited with the three of us is intense and moving.

Yoka remembers the mixed emotions she felt coming home after the war. Although she had been lovingly cared for in her war-time family, consisting of her "Aunt" Ella, her "Uncle" Dick, and her baby "sister" Roos, she was happy to be back in her own home, with her own father, sister and brother. But that home had been permanently and profoundly changed. The longing and expectations of three years spent in hiding could not possibly be fulfilled by any reality, let alone the reality of a home without Hilde.

Fran's experiences while she was in hiding had been difficult. While Jan and Fen Barens were politically courageous and risked their lives to save Jews and do other work for the underground, they did not understand children. Too young to understand what was happening, Fran, five years old at the time, was often severely punished and even beaten for childish misbehavior. In Amsterdam, the Barens lived two doors down from the Hollandse Schouwburg, the theater which was used as the detainment center for Jews who had been rounded up and were on their way to Westerbork. Fran was frequently awakened at night as, outside her bedroom window, noisy trucks rolled up to load or unload their terror-stricken passengers. No doubt Hilde, too, passed under that window.

Otto, three years old when he left home, had no pre-war memories. His war-time family, Hopperus Buma, had been very good to him. Still he could hardly be expected to be a "normal" six-year-old by the time he returned home. Otto loved being reunited with Gerrit and frequently expressed his love, and also perhaps his fear of losing Gerrit again. Each day he asked Gerrit what time he would be coming home from work. His idea of supreme happiness was for him and Gerrit to go to sleep at the same time one evening. Gerrit tried to be both mother and father to the three of us and take care of many pressing business problems at the same time. He hoped to marry again in order to provide a mother for our family. Meanwhile the problems were many.

One major problem was Gerrit's pre-war partner in the bicycle factory, van den Berg. Van den Berg, who was not Jewish, had been in charge of the Magneet factory during the war. After the war he tried to keep Gerrit from getting the factory back. This kind of behavior towards Jews who returned from the camps or from hiding was regrettably not uncommon. At one point, van den Berg made the outrageous accusation that Gerrit had done business with the Germans. As a result the Dutch authorities detained Gerrit for several weeks while the charges were being investigated. Yoka's first post-war birthday fell during the time Gerrit was being detained, and it was only with great difficulty that he obtained permission to go home to celebrate this first family birthday after liberation. The charges were eventually dismissed, but this injustice coming on top of the suffering inflicted by the Germans, profoundly embittered Gerrit. It was the proverbial last straw and no doubt contributed to his developing the cancer that killed him.

In December 1946, Gerrit and the three children emigrated to the United States. When we arrived, Gerrit was already ill, though his disease had not yet been diagnosed. He never recovered. After his death in October 1947, Gerrit's sister Jo and her husband Barend became our legal guardians. Jo kept her promises to our father to take care of us. This was not always easy, because Barend had no interest in raising us, and his business kept him and Jo abroad for many months at a time. Thus our odyssey did not end. We spent periods of time living with various relatives and friends, sometimes together, sometimes apart, sometimes cared for with affection, sometimes with indifference at best.

In spite of it all, we grew up. Today Otto lives in Colorado with his wife, Daisy, the daughter of Jewish survivors from Salonica, Greece. They have two young sons, Gerald, named after his grandfather Gerrit, and David. Otto is a systems analyst with a computer firm. Fran is an artist living in Maryland with her husband, Robert. Robert, too, was born in Holland, and our two families knew each other before the war. He and his family escaped by way of the former Dutch East Indies. Fran and Robert have three grown daughters and one granddaughter. Yoka did not marry. She lived in Israel for many years, returned to Holland for a time, and now makes her home in California. She taught English literature here and abroad and is now a psychotherapist.

Sometimes we wonder what our lives would have been like if there had been no Hitler, no war, no persecution, no policy of annihilation. We will never know. The letters that follow describe how our family, like hundreds of thousands of other ordinary families leading ordinary lives, tried to deal with the cataclysmic events that overwhelmed us.

                                    Leeuwarden, April 24th, 1945
Dear Suze, René, and children,
    Last week I wrote you a letter from Heerenveen, where I am living now, but I only mailed that letter yesterday because I was hoping to find somebody who could take

it along. I had just mailed it when I heard last night that there was a man from Brussels here with a car (I'm staying in Leeuwarden for a couple of days visiting old friends with whom I was in hiding) and now I'll look up that man and ask him if he will take the letter along. I hope it can be done. In that case you will receive the mailed letter later on, but it contains approximately the same information.

I have fared all right. I have been in hiding since September 30th, 1943, that is now more than a year and a half, and I'm breathing more freely now. I last heard from the children more than a month ago and at that time all was well with them. Otto is in Diepenveen near Deventer, now also a liberated area. I recently received a little note from him, written by his foster parents, and I was very happy with it. But that was dated April 4th, still before the liberation. I hope and expect that he is well because not much fighting took place there and the people with whom he is staying are first class and very calm and sensible. Yoka is in Zuid Holland with a mayor and his small family (one young child), also very good, but that area has not yet been liberated. According to a message received about the middle of March, everything was still all right. Fransje is in Amsterdam with a couple without children, also exceptionally nice and good people. They managed reasonably well with food. In any case, a woman from around here visited them by bike in March and she said that Frans, the darling, looked cheerful and healthy and fortunately still well fed. But still I often worry about her. I hope that it will all work out all right. Yoka and Otto are also doing well as far as food is concerned because they live near large farms, and as you know, that always makes a big difference. I have already reserved a car and will get a permit to drive there immediately following the liberation of Holland. I will also take food along for various families, which I can get from some friendly farmers, and I will load up the car with it. I will pick Otto up on the way. What a reunion after almost three years!!!

With Hilde, unfortunately things went amiss. That was a great misfortune and I often reproach myself although I cannot say where I should have acted differently, and yet sometimes I do. But so often she would not do what I thought best. At the end of September 1943, I was away on a trip for a couple of days when they suddenly rounded up the last Jews of Amsterdam and sent them to Westerbork. Hilde was at home with Father and Mother. Wednesday morning, September 29th, around eight o'clock, they were forced to leave the house; I heard about this in the country. When I returned to the city in the evening, they were already in Westerbork and I couldn't enter the house anymore. Because the three children had been in hiding then already for a year and a half, I did not visit Hil, but tried, with the help of friends, to arrange for her to escape. It would certainly have succeeded, but she did not want to. She was afraid (we could exchange letters which were smuggled in and out) that if she were to flee, reprisals would be taken against the parents and that they would be placed on a penal transport. Four times we tried to convince her, each time somebody went into the camp with an entry permit, but she did not want to do it. At first I insisted as strongly as possible that she should come (it always did succeed, others escaped) but when she absolutely refused, none of us could do anything about it. She wrote that she wanted to wait until the parents had been put on a transport, and then she would come out. Sadly, however, she fell ill, jaundice, and had to go to the hospital in the camp. The nursing care was very good there because of all the Jewish doctors and nurses, but, as bad luck would have it, suddenly on February 7th, 1944, five hundred patients were placed on transport and she was among them. On February 8th she crossed the border and nothing more has been heard from her. I fear the worst, but I still have some hope that she will return, because she has courage, if only she regained her health. I heard that she was sent to Riesa, to a camp. That is between Leipzig and Dresden, but where could she possibly be now after fourteen months? I hardly dare to think about it, and how the poor soul must yearn for the children, and her uncertainty about how our trio is doing. Until February '44 I wrote her at least once a week so she knew that until then all was well. When I went into hiding I had arranged with a good friend to send her food, but Siemons took over that task, you remember, an acquaintance of Barend. To my great horror I heard from Hil, after two months, when I got her first letters at the end of November, that she had never received anything. After inquiry I found out that "Mister" Siemons had *forgotten* about it, imagine, it had slipped his mind. From my hiding place I arranged for a new connection and fortunately was able to supply her with plenty of food during the next six weeks. There was also more than sufficient for Father and Mother and my parents-in-law. Details are not important, but Hil received everything and wrote me that it was more than enough. I hope that it strengthened her because jaundice makes you terribly weak and the camp food was inadequate.

Mother and Father were also put on the transport of February 8th, 1944, and, I am fairly sure, went to Zelle near Hannover (now liberated). They had a so-called *"Austausch"* stamp, a stamp which the Nazis gave to Jews who had good connections in England or America. Those Jews were then, so-to-speak, hoarded up in order to be exchanged for Nazis (civilians) who were, for example, taken prisoner in North Africa and later in France. Therefore I have a bit more hope for them. In the last year a fair number of Jews from Zelle have already been exchanged, also to Palestine. Maybe you have already heard something about this. In any case Zelle was not such a horrendous camp as the others, according to those Jews who were released and have arrived in neutral territory. Let us hope that we may see all three of them again, otherwise it would be just too terrible.

How are all of you getting along? Let me know as soon

as possible, and also how Jops and Lien and Ben and Barend and the children are. I don't have an address in America but I'm sure that you will write to them. And when you write me back, give me their address so that I can notify them as soon as I know more. Jacqui will have become quite a young lady by now and Jetty has been engaged for some time. I am longing so for you. One time I almost had a chance to be smuggled across the Rhine, and I imagined how surprised you would be if I suddenly were to ring your door bell and appear before you. But I am glad that it didn't work out, because now I feel more united with the children and I don't like the idea that I am already liberated and Yoka and Fransje are not. I would have preferred to be the last one in line. But at least I was not the first, because by then Otto was already free. I received such good and reassuring news from their foster parents. The children were three, five and seven years old when they went into hiding. Now they are six, eight and ten. I still see them the way they were then; I will be surprised when I see them again. But I'm not concerned, and I'm sure that I will quickly regain their confidence. I will have to control myself and not force myself on them. But that will work out all right and I trust my intuition to find the right approach. In any case, we never really lost contact because we constantly exchanged letters. When you read them later on, those letters from the children, you will enjoy them, regardless of all the misery. They were the reason that I was able to get through the misery relatively well.

We have now been liberated for a week and it already seems like months. Below I am giving you two addresses. One in Heerenveen where I am staying until I can go to Amsterdam. The other one is my friend in Amsterdam. When Amsterdam is liberated write me there, but that may take several more weeks.

Now I am going to try to give this letter to that fellow. I don't know him but I know his hotel. In case he isn't there anymore I will find another way.

1945

We must, as I already wrote in that other letter, see each other very, very often in the future. Let us hope that we will be together again very soon.

Greetings and many kisses,

your Gait

c/o Mrs. T. Dam
Geruischloozeweg 304
Oranjewoud, Heerenveen Fr.
(temporary address)

c/o Mr. J.H. Barens
Plantage Middenlaan 20a
Amsterdam C.

Hilversum, July 14, 1945

Dear Jops and Barend,

It is Saturday afternoon and a beautiful summer day. We have just finished picking all the apples off the tree in our yard. Albert[1] stood on a big double ladder we had borrowed from Jaarsma, the neighbor across the way, and I stood on a chair to receive the apples. Then Yoka, Frans and Otto were allowed to place them in a large basket, each in turn. Each of the children was also allowed to climb up the ladder once, but not very high, and to pick the apples from the tree by themselves. They like eating them even better if they happen to find one that's already good and ripe. And now we have a big basketful, well over one hundred. You will have no trouble picturing that little scene, but you can't imagine what a wonderful sight it was to look down from my chair into these three healthy, tanned, uplifted faces—sometimes I had to wait a bit because they were discussing whose turn it was to take the apple from me!

I am now sitting in the front of the house, in the room off to the side, typing and looking out over the Trompenbergerweg. The past three years—or five, if you will—are not even like a nightmare; they were that only while they lasted. They are like something unreal and, except for some of the more powerful experiences, I sometimes have to make an effort in order to remember what everything was like. I received your June 24th letter at the beginning of the week at Huter's and the July 2nd letter got here today. So now I know that you received my April letter to Suze. I think that in it I more or less told you what happened to Hilde. What a terrible pity that it should have struck her of all people, poor soul, for she belonged with us. I even wrote her at Westerbork that if she should not be around later, nothing would be the same. But she could not be induced to flee the camp before she knew for sure that her parents had gone to Theresienstadt. But then she herself fell ill, with jaundice, and was admitted to the sick barracks where Father was as well. During the night of February 7, 1943, all of the sick and their healthy kin were suddenly ordered to leave, and so Mother had to go, too. Hil had been visited at least three or four times by people from the organization determined to pull her out (that never failed, dozens managed to leave that way!), but she always said that she wanted to wait a little longer. That's what she wrote me too, for until the last days we regularly exchanged letters that had been smuggled out. I still have them. Later I thought that I should have written: you out or me in. But Siem says that in my entire life I had never yet succeeded in making Hil do anything against her will, and I would not have succeeded then. That's how I feel about it too, and if I had gone there (as I had originally thought of doing, although not eagerly) I most likely would have decided to wait with her and wouldn't now be picking apples with the children. As far as our dear mother and father are concerned, I am not altogether blameless. Those wretched souls left everything to me and I was afraid to let them go into hiding. Had I dared they would still be here, but I thought, along with nearly everyone else at the time, that a stamp for Zelle was better than constant fear and the danger of hiding. I managed to keep them in the Breughelstraat until the end of September

1943, but then things went wrong. I myself happened to be in Westerbork on behalf of the J.R. [Jewish Council] and at one a.m. heard that Amsterdam was being cleared out; at the time there were still some 5,000 Jews there. I waited until one in the afternoon to meet their train but it still hadn't shown up. I could still leave the camp that day and thought about the children and that I would always be able to re-enter the camp but probably never leave it again if I didn't do it then. So I said to one of Hil's good friends that I was leaving, and she asked me what I was still doing there and said that Hil wouldn't want it any other way. There was a truck in the camp which was going to Rotterdam. I hitched a ride to Amersfoort, pulled the star off as soon as I left the camp (never to wear it again) and arrived in Amsterdam by train. That was Wednesday, October [sic] 29, 1943. At eight o'clock that morning Mother, Father, and Hil had been taken from their home, as were my in-laws and the entire Jewish Council, including Asscher and Cohen. Your parents, Barend, had already been sent to Westerbork a few months earlier but Mo claimed to have received assurances that they would never be sent to Germany. For that matter, he had the same assurance for Daan's wife and daughters, but all of them were deported anyway, although not until September '44. Daan's wife and daughters are now back in Holland. The past few months they have been living in Amsterdam, very near to us, and I was friendly with them and we frequently chatted.

Mother and Father understood very well why you didn't come to say goodbye. We received your message from Lyon and later from Barcelona, and Barend's last postcard with its "So long and all the best" arrived in November 1942. Then, in December, we learned from the radio that a ship with 143 Dutch emigrants had arrived in America or thereabouts, and we knew that you were among them. We were overcome with joy and Mother and Father were enormously relieved; and when we got the letters from Lien we knew a lot more. You can imagine how happy we were, and the only thing that bothered me was that your joy could not be complete because all of you naturally worried about us.

As for me, most of the time I had the feeling that nothing would happen to me. Still, there were times I had my doubts and sometimes I even came close to despair. And poor Hil was absolutely convinced that she would pull through, but when the moment of decision arrived she was incapable of takingresponsibility for her own fate, and her high moral principles got in the way and led her to sacrifice herself for her parents. She feared reprisals; that if she escaped, her parents would be sent to Poland with a punitive transport (I was told that she didn't go through with it because of both our parents). I know now that this almost certainly would not have happened and at that time too we wrote her this often enough. In this case she was too conscientious about what she considered to be her principal duty. What a pity; I would have been so very happy for her had she made it—and she deserved it more than I.

After liberation, as soon as I was allowed to do so, I traveled from Oranjewoud (that's where I was during the last months, how could Barend know!!!) to Westerbork and looked at the lists myself. I was still hoping that Father and Mother had been sent to Zelle and Hil to another camp in Germany. That's what friends had told me. But the lists could not be clearer. They had been sent to Auschwitz with the transport of the sick and I don't have to tell you the rest. Of this entire sick transport not a single person has come back so far; in all probability the end came immediately upon arrival and that is something for which we should probably be grateful.

During the entire year and a half that I was in hiding I was sure of one thing: Hil would come back. But during the last months I realized that hunger posed a great danger because they [the Germans] had other things to worry about than to keep on supplying the Jewish camps with food. I never did believe that it would end in a deliberate, carefully planned system of annihilation—until after the liberation.

1945

Then I knew better. I still vividly recall, dear Jops, what you once told me during the last days: "Never in a German camp." You were right. But with Hil I wasn't able to prevent it, and the reason we did not go into hiding sooner is due to other factors. In my own mind I know that I bear no guilt (relatively speaking, as always).

I think you left in July and that same month we found a place for the children outside the city. Nico and Lien Hamburger and their children were, as you probably know, picked up in a raid that same month; Michel Speijer and his wife and child plucked from their hideout through betrayal; Bolo and his brothers waited long enough for all three to be sent to Vught, and later, also in September 1943, to Westerbork, to which the women were sent as well. Only the daughter, Lilly, returned; the rest is unknown, and so. . . . The Koords also gone, with the children; Wim and Else and their children. . .well in Amsterdam but I haven't talked to them yet. But I did talk to Fie and E. They had the most beautiful hiding place I had ever seen: in the vaccination center behind the Artis[2] aquarium, where there was a little house between the sheds and no one ever came or would think of looking for people.

Fritz Goudsmit is back too, so Barend can play bridge as soon as he gets here. Zeldenrust is fine and his son has come back, which is wonderful. With tuberculosis, to be sure, but the doctor says he'll get over it in a year. Cis Vis, both husband and wife, are okay too; Geri Sluizer and wife (those favorites of yours!) are back as well, Geri after having spent a long time in Auschwitz (picked up in Brussels). Berthold Gersons is back from Theresienstadt, by way of Odessa, but there is no news about his wife and boy. Nathan Dasberg and wife and all the children came safely back from their hiding places. (He had shaved off his beard, which has since grown back.)[3]

There are a thousand and one details to relate about everything that's happened. To give an example: in November 1943 I learned from Rachel Nutkewitz that it was pos-

Signs of Life

sible to go to Portugal legally. One of her acquaintances knew about it. So I tried to find out more. It would be legal, with a large bus and twenty couples at 50,000 guilders per couple, a bit more with the children. I thought it must be true, what with the amount being so high, and started to think about ways of raising the money. I succeeded, that is to say, I could get hold of it through business relations. I discussed it with Hil who had just been away visiting the children for a few days. She said, literally: "Don't waste your time, I don't want to go to Portugal and I am not going to Portugal, and I wouldn't go even if you paid me to!" And that, mind you, at a time when the deportations were in full swing. She didn't even want to hear more about it. Even so, I went on with my inquiries, for I wasn't about to risk a recurrence of what happened to me in the beginning of 1940. But I didn't think it was safe enough and nothing came of it. It appeared to be a legal journey organized by the Germans whose outcome was uncertain. But Hil always thought: next month it will be over. Only later, when it was too late and I wrote to her that it was a question of a few months, she wrote back that she was sure it would take longer than that. That was in January '44. She never did grasp the seriousness of the situation, I know that now, and by trying to ignore the war and the occupation she got totally confused, which prevented her from making the practical decisions that had to be made. Except of course the decision to send the children into hiding; but that was my express wish because I could find no peace as long as they were with me in a house that could be raided at any moment. Others, Rudi Gersons for example, had their children leave their hiding places so that they could be placed on an exemption list together. I never even considered that. I was on many exemption lists (which protected Hil as well), but I never once mentioned the children on any of the forms we had to fill out for this. The Germans didn't even know we had children. We always stated: no children. All this time Frans stayed with the same people, a husband and wife with no children of their own. They first lived in Zandvoort but in January '43 came to Amsterdam, with Frans—in the Plantage Middenlaan no less, two houses down from the Schouwburg (oh, yes, perhaps you don't know this. The Hollandsche Schouwburg served as a collection point for Jews to be sent to Westerbork).

At the time Hil said that she didn't want to go to Portugal (which of course meant leaving legally with the children—like Teddy Korijn and others, for example), she was trying to buy a fake identity card for me from the son-in-law of an acquaintance of hers. She had paid three hundred guilders for it but it never materialized. Instead of telling me (I had told her that I would get one myself if I thought it necessary; after all, I had obtained one for her too), she went to Café Formosa one Friday, around November 10, 1942. There she had an interview. When she left and was about to board the streetcar she was promptly arrested. The guy was an agent provocateur! They locked her up in the central office of Jewish affairs in the Marnixstraat Police Station, but I heard about it that same evening and Sunday morning went to see her. They took her out of the cell and we talked a few hours in the room reserved for lawyers and their clients while two detectives whom I knew stood watch. I had taken all kinds of things with me and daily sent her packages and a few times went there myself. The detectives didn't work for the Jewish department and knew me through my business. We immediately got busy trying to get Hil out and succeeded in keeping her in the Marnixstraat, where she was treated well, until just before Christmas. (She was allowed to leave her cell during the day to play bridge in a sunny room with other Jews, among whom Mr. Joosten from the Prins Hendrikkade who had been in hiding in Friesland and had been betrayed.) But then she had to go to Westerbork anyway. Thereupon I managed to get myself appointed as courier to Westerbork, which was connected with my work in supplying the camps with food (I was in charge of this, and we sent enormous quantities of extra food, bought at outrageous black market prices, that is to say the money was black because the Germans didn't permit it, but we managed to get it delivered at normal prices because all the suppliers cooperated), and I went to Westerbork once a week. You should have seen Hil's face the first time I arrived with the night train; Hil knew that I was coming and was waiting for me as the train entered the camp. The first time that happened was in February '43. At that time she stayed in the camp until June, when she was released thanks to my job with the Jewish Council. Exactly ten days later both of us were picked up on a Friday evening in the Breughelstraat. It was a punitive measure because of some transgression of the Jewish Council. They rounded up all those who had been recently released, this time with their families. It was a Friday night and a night I shall never forget. Mother and Father had to go too. Poor Hil was shaking and I gave her some Hoffmann drops and she calmed down. There were a "Gruene" [German Police] and an NSB-man [Dutch Nazi Party]. I talked for an hour with the Gruene (who was the boss), after which Mother and Father, who were already in bed, were allowed to stay home. I was as calm as I am now as I write this. That night more than six hundred people were rounded up and no one else, not even the very sick, were permitted to remain at home. I said "See you" to Mother and Father, for I knew that I would be back. Indeed, after two weeks I was back in Amsterdam, free for the time being, and Hil got out in September. Hil could have gotten out four weeks earlier, but she couldn't stand Amsterdam—a paved nightmare, she said—and would rather be in Westerbork. . . .if only there were no danger of deportation. And so, around September 23, 1943, we were both back in the Breughelstraat. On Monday, September 27, I absolutely had to go to Westerbork. It wasn't even my turn as courier but my father-in-law had to have a letter and I had to speak with someone urgently. So I bribed another courier with a suit of clothes to let me go in his place and that's why I am sitting here now typing. Chance played a

1945

big part in this, or maybe a lucky star. I certainly could tell you a lot about my luck during the time I was in hiding but that would take too long. The people in Drente, where I also hid out for ten months, used to say, "Uncle Gerrit has a sixth sense," because time and time again I could sense when to move on, and three times the "Gruenen" arrived just after I had flown the coop. And then they took others instead, those who had made fun of me at first or in any case hadn't listened to me.

But I digress. Now you're brought up to date a bit. Oh, yes, I just remembered that in your letter you asked about Jo Arens. Yesterday he was in Hilversum and called me in Weesp and practically cried tears of joy that he was able to call me again from my own home. My first question was: how's the family, and all of them are fine, that is to say, his wife and children. I then asked: do you have enough money and that he did. From which you can gather that I am managing. Thanks for your sincere offer, Barend. Even if you hadn't mentioned it at all, I still would have known that I could always count on you. But it was good to know that you're doing all right. Have heard nothing from Eva and Barend. Jo Velleman and wife and son have surfaced—I don't know why I thought of that all of a sudden. Jops, a letter of yours lies on each side of the typewriter and I see your name twice. To realize that you are ALIVE and that we shall see each other again is an indescribably joyful sensation— and that the children will see you too and you them! It would certainly act as a tonic on Lien. I don't quite understand the situation with her. You write that she isn't very strong. But what exactly is the matter and how come Albert doesn't have a letter yet? Is everything all right with her? And how are they doing financially? Please let me know a little more about them, because it rather worries me that you write so vaguely about Lien and Ben. But I forget that you can't write such long letters all at once and so I'll wait for the next piece of mail.

I started out writing to you about Frans. She is eight

Signs of Life

now and stayed with the same people, who took excellent care of her, until the liberation. Imagine, despite the lack of food in Amsterdam they never went without butter on their bread. No wonder Frans looked very well and weighed sixty pounds. Very cute and a sweet and unusually pretty face. Her front teeth protrude a bit but the dentist is taking care of that. I immediately re-enrolled her in the Godelinde-school in Hilversum. We've been living here for two weeks now (or is it three already?), and after spending a few weeks in the second grade they put her in the third and she is very proud. In Amsterdam she didn't go to school until the liberation, so everything was very strange to her, but she had been tutored at home and was quite up to date. She often went to Artis where she was always allowed to ride the camel back to its stall, which is the longest ride of all.

In May I picked up Otto while I was living in Oranje-woud. He was staying in an enormous house in Diepenveen near Deventer. Wonderful people, Hopperus Buma. I stayed there with him for a week and then took him back with me to Friesland because we couldn't go to Holland yet.[4] I'll tell you about our reunion some other time. He has become a sturdy little lad, very intelligent and very sweet. He clings to me in such a way that it scares me sometimes; I think he positively idolizes his own father. When, during the first days, we went walking in the woods of Diepenveen he never let go of my hand and called out to all acquaintances we met on the way: "You know who this is? This is my *father!*" And he said it with such intense pride and happiness in his voice that it warmed my heart and gave me the shivers at the same time. We slept together in one room and in the morning he crawled into my bed and we played. His life was suddenly complete; no matter how well he had been looked after, this was his OWN father. We remained another month in Oranjewoud and only then were we able to travel to the central part of Holland.

All kinds of locally significant things happened, little things about which I'll tell you more later. I just want to mention this: When I was at the city hall in Heerenveen (I had already made the acquaintance of the mayor and the town clerk earlier), an official suddenly said: "Oh, but you must be Mr. Verdoner. If that's the case, two weeks ago there was a telegram for you from America." I asked why they hadn't tried me at home since my address in Oranjewoud was registered with the office charged with locating those who had been in hiding. "We had heard that you had already left," they said. And then they showed me their first reply to Barend, that is, to the consul in New York. I said: "Now at least Mr. Broekman himself knows that in 1910 he moved to the Sarphatiepark in Amsterdam"[5]—and I rather let them have it (I have become very tough!). And then I demanded a new telegram despite the fact that the post office was already closed and made them go with me to the supervisor, who personally accepted my telegram even though I had to sign as "mayor," but that was no problem.

Then I left for Hilversum by taxi with Otto and all the luggage. Left Oranjewoud at 4:00 a.m. and arrived in Hilversum at 9:00. At eleven I was at the Military Authority and the Political Tracing Service (P.O.D.) to discuss van den Berg. Influential military friends that I had made in Friesland gave me excellent introductions to the highest authorities—I only had to show these to their subordinates and everything was fine. It took me five days to collect and organize the material against van den berg, after which Siem helped me put it together. But Siem drew up the declaration by himself, which he is so good at. I did the rest myself and doors opened all over the Military Authority and the P.O.D. and I had a tremendous amount of cooperation. The speed with which I was able to take care of everything is a miracle over here. The day after I filed my complaint, two armed men came to pick the scoundrel up, took him straight through Weesp, right to the prisoners barracks. I mean he was hauled from the office. Details to follow. Never in my life have I been surer of anything succeeding than this. And everyone, even Siem and Kinebanian and

Witkamp, was afraid that he would be set free again because last September he started protecting his rear and cultivating people in the underground. But I didn't pay any attention to that and was willing to bet anyone that I would get him locked up but good. Throughout the week that I was preparing my case, the political police constantly asked me: "When are you going to hand this crook over to us, Mr. Verdoner?" And yet you must have a rock-solid case and incontrovertible evidence if you want to put him away in such a manner that no lawyer in the world will be able to get him out. Because, don't forget, he was never a member of the NSB—he was too clever for that, at least that's what he thought.

He has already been in prison for three weeks and his file is like the proverbial tree, growing thicker and thicker. He has been involved in all kinds of shady business and is going to jail for various offenses, all of which I can pin on him. The fact that he has profited from the German occupation and harmed others—or even attempted to do this—for that alone the penalty is fifteen years!! On top of that I can prove collaboration of the worst possible sort: robbing Magneet of between fifty and one hundred thousand guilders!! which I don't think I'll have trouble proving. According to his tax return his capital before the war consisted of 17,000 guilders. This oaf had left a completely itemized property statement at the office, prepared in his own hand, which showed assets amounting to two hundred thousand!! Everything earned off the books. Speaking of black market, etc., it is heavily punished too—with total confiscation, according to the latest government communication.

Immediately after his arrest I was appointed Director of Magneet by the Commission for the Restoration of Justice and Administration in Hilversum (which covers the municipality of Weesp). Van den berg was disqualified by law, so that now I am entirely in charge and am rid of the scoundrel for good. Witkamp is again in charge of the office and Siem is my adviser. I am great friends with him and like him much better than ever before (at one time I had almost broken off relations with him, but things were different from what I thought, which makes me very happy because I like him a lot).

I already have eighteen people working at jobs for the Military Authority, specifically at fixing up bicycles that had been requisitioned by the Germans for distribution to the public. That will take me at least four months and I will also recoup the overhead. In addition, Vasteland is going to be suing Fokker for large-scale indemnification, and eventually Magneet too will go against Fokker. Magneet, as you may know, is no longer housed in the old factory, which stands completely empty. In September '44 they struck again, hauling away all of the woodworking machines, and it's like a shell there. I think I'll ask for a huge amount (a couple of hundred thousand) and Siem agrees because the damage certainly warrants it. By the way, all of van den Berg's (why not give him a capital letter this time, that's about all he'll have left) assets have been inventoried and frozen, including his personal property. I took care of that and an administrator has been appointed by the government. They themselves can't get their hands on it anymore. All of Weesp enjoyed it immensely—the old employees most of all. Enough about that, the rest I'll tell you one of these days in person. At any rate, it's a complete victory of justice (represented by the undersigned) over a crook. . . . I strayed from the subject when I got to my arrival in Hilversum. That same Friday we traveled to Amsterdam, stayed there two nights and then continued, with Otto and Frans, on to Weesp where we stayed one week with the Witkamps. The reunion of Otto and Frans was a little tepid, as was to be expected from children who no longer know one another. But now, after so many weeks, they are getting on famously, much like a brother and sister are supposed to behave. Frans was very happy to be with me, although the first couple of days I wasn't much good to her because I was so incredibly busy with the Weesp business. But after that I managed to win my "Frankie" back and she became mine even more completely than she had been before. In short, she is a real sweetheart.

And now Yoka. She was in Woubrugge near Alphen-on-the-Rhine, living in the mayor's house. Another huge house and right on the water. Come, see, and convince yourself what a darling she has become, and how pretty! She is in the sixth grade and one of the best students (except for arithmetic, barely passing). Such a dear and so sensitive. Jo, you just have to see them soon, and you'll enjoy yourself no end. It's a threesome you'll have fun with. Yes, Jops, I always knew for sure that if something were to happen to me you would make a new home for my three children and care for them as if they were your own—and that Barend would go along. I was as certain of that as if both of you had told me directly. This knowledge gave me great strength all the time I was in hiding. But now you have to make sure that the children don't see less of you and miss out on account of my return. I certainly hope that we will not be separated again for the rest of our lives. Best of all I'd like to have two houses under one roof, for then I would know for sure that the children won't be deprived of you. When I told her you were preparing packages for them, Yoka said right away: "Oh, if Aunt Jo is sending packages then it's got to be okay." Of the three, Yoka remembers the most, which is to be expected. Some day I'll tell you what she said about Hil. She and Otto miss her. But Yoka doesn't talk about it; Otto does, in a most natural way.

Thus Yoka was in Woubrugge. And I had a house in Hilversum that stood completely empty, a dirty house with a neglected yard, but no one yet to work on it. Yet I wanted the children to be together and with me as soon as possible and have them get used to a regular routine. So I went to see our faithful Toos, who in the meanwhile had married Pros and had a child of almost two, which I already knew. Toos and her family now live in the upstairs frontroom, that is to say, it is a bed-sitting room for Toos and Pros. Their child sleeps upstairs. Yoka and Frans again have their own room, charmingly furnished (they are crazy about it) and Otto has a fine room on the second floor where he used to sleep before. I myself sleep in our old room with the old green furniture; and now Albert is here too and sleeps next to me. In addition, there is a live-in maid. . . . I told Toos and Pros: it may be for one, two or six months, in any case it's temporary until I find a permanent arrangement for my family. But they were very happy with the arrangement (they had been living with her parents), and my problem was solved for the time being. And I must say, it's working out well, and Toos is reliable and good to the children. They have been to Crailoo pool with her and the maid a number of times (they have seven weeks vacation, can you believe it!) and all three are taking swimming lessons dangling from a rod. When they know how to swim we'll visit the island for a few days (it's back in my possession, with the cottage) and really have a good time. I hope that Albert can go along. He can invite his friends too. . . . My in-laws are back in Amsterdam and living for the time being in an apartment owned by Emmy de Vries (wife of Sam de Vries, a cousin of my mother-in-law, who is also dead). They still look rather thin but she hasn't changed and sometimes calls me dear (yuck), at least the first couple of times on the telephone. He's very depressed and they now know that Otto died a year ago in Belsen, and my father-in-law suspects it about Hil although he doesn't say anything. My mother-in-law at any rate still seems to have hope. My father-in-law asked me if I still had hope and I told him: no, not any longer. He will have to know some time although we will probably never have any more news. I put him in touch with a very tough P.O.D. man (political tracing service), an old connection of mine from the Marnixstraat, who'll be going after his property for him and this makes him very happy. For, although some trams have begun running, the service is still limited. Just this week we got two hours of electricity in

Signs of Life

Hilversum, just enough to run the vacuum cleaner, but we don't need light. The food is fairly decent and in any case sufficient. But butter is still hard to get and we get a lard supplement. The children get the butter. I brought back plenty of good cheese from Friesland and they also gave me a good-sized ham and a large chunk of dried bacon and some eggs. The people I stayed with are tremendous; I'll tell you more about them later. —— The dashes mean that there has been a break for a few hours. I was with the children in the backyard and connected a hose we had borrowed to our sprinkler; then all of us in bathing suits began squirting one another with water and had a great time; and Yoka secretly shut off the water and I had to look inside the hose, and then she turned the water back on to spray me; in short, it was a really pleasant morning and no one wants to leave the house because we are having such a good time. Then we hid two apples in the yard, that is, I hid them and the children had to find and eat them. After that we ate bread with sardines (which some English officer friends had given me back in Friesland) and corned beef from the same source. This afternoon I'll surprise them with canned prunes topped with condensed milk substituting for cream—we still had a few cans from before the war that had been stored with Karl Brandt together with some canned vegetables and such. Despite the food shortage in Hilversum, he never touched them and returned them to me when I came back. I asked him if he and his children would rather have starved to death than open them up. He said, no, he wouldn't go that far but that it was a question of honor to return the stuff to me. And I replied that that was very decent and said: thanks a lot, thinking in the meantime: you should have eaten them all the same, fellow, because when I was in the north and didn't lack for anything—yes, even had an egg daily with my breakfast—I thought of Hilversum where it was even worse than in Amsterdam (except for firewood, seeing that they cut down half the woods) and thought: I'm glad they still have those few scraps of food we left with them, and then, good God, everything is returned to you and you have to say: how very decent! or else they would be disappointed in the bargain, and their self-control entirely for nought. But, anyhow, because of that the children will be eating canned prunes this afternoon, including Brandt's little daughter. And our linen supply too virtually remained untouched, that is the linen cupboard with its contents, and also the front room furniture with bookcase and the books, although the furniture is rather worn. But the three Deventer carpets turned up too and the moths hadn't gotten to them. For the rest, all the carpets are gone, including the ones in the hall and the bedrooms. For the time being I have put the small rugs that were stored at Siem's in the children's rooms. Siem and Tilly and Pem had kept everything very nicely, even the silver that they were eager to get rid of because of the employees. The silver has been put away in four safes here in the Bank of Amsterdam, where I am being treated like a king because I am on friendly terms with Mr. André de la Porte, who is the director in Amsterdam and who was very nice to me during the war. For that reason he'll get the Magneet account, which he seems to fancy quite a bit. He's already offered us unrestricted credit in case we need it, which I doubt; he rather regrets that because the bank would like to make some money, too. But in any case, the director of the Hilversum branch also heads the Military Authority's financial department for the Gooi region and is a very good business connection, always eager to be of service, and there have been times I've taken him up on it. Since the liberation I never show up at offical agencies in Friesland without excellent introductions to whoever is in charge, and I get these without fail.

So the van den bergs took off with my Buick, that is, they had v.d.b.'s brother ostensibly requisition the last of Magneet's Buicks (they had sold the others a few years ago, with part of the proceeds no doubt disappearing as "black" money into their personal account). This brother is a lieutenant with the Royal Electrical and Mechanical Engineers (REME) in Breda, from which he made a special trip to pick up the car when I claimed it for Magneet and they saw that they would have to give it back. And now practically the entire Hilversum Military Authority is busy trying to get the car returned to me, for it feels that its authority has been flouted since it had ordered v.d.b. (the family, that is, because after all he is behind bars) via Weesp to turn the car over to Magneet. And no doubt that won't be the end of it because they are now looking for this lieutenant v.d. berg because he had no authority to requisition, besides operating out of his area, and so he won't be a lieutenant much longer, if the punishment isn't worse. And the Military Authority has written out a standing order to take possession of the car no matter where, and so this week you'll get to see Gait riding around in the Buick again, which will be a real relief because it's almost impossible to do without it. On the other hand, it's also kind of too bad, because I'll no longer be bicycling 40 to 50 km a day as I've been doing until now, sometimes even 70 km, when I had to go to Amsterdam on Jack v.d.b.'s lightweight Magneet. And that did my body a world of good. I feel completely fit, strong and healthy, and better than before the war. I sleep very well and rise early. My mind is fresh, clear and sharper than ever. Am more decisive and do what my gut tells me is right and brook no interference once my mind is made up, no matter what. Three weeks ago, in a meeting with Siem, Kinebanian and Witkamp, I didn't agree with any one of them or the three of them put together, but I stuck to my guns and, as has now been irrefutably borne out, correctly so. So you'll be seeing a slightly improved version of Gait when we meet again. I no longer have any excess fat on my body, but that's not on account of the food, which was nourishing enough, but due to the exercise I've been getting these past months. I haven't put back the thirty pounds I lost in the first months of the war and I now weigh 143 pounds, slim as can be but with a lot more stamina and less

1945

73

need of sleep!!! The stomach is holding up fine, although I sometimes had trouble when I was in hiding. Nerves had something to do with it, I suppose. . . . For me the main thing is this: I want to live near you with the children. I don't know yet whether Europe's future is such that it will be safe to raise the children here; it remains to be seen; we'll probably know in a couple of years. But I don't want them to run the risk of later experiencing what happened to us. And I would feel a lot better about Palestine if it were situated in America or South Africa. Right now it seems to me too much of a future crisis area, what with all that oil and the Suez Canal and the Russians on one side and the English on the other. Best of all I'd like to remain in Hilversum where it is so very beautiful, with lakes that soon will be such a great source of enjoyment for the children too. But we'll talk about all this quietly later on. I suddenly recall your words, Barend, when the call-ups came and you spent one night thinking about what to do. You told me then: if we don't flee we'll certainly go to Poland; if we do flee there is a chance we may not go to Poland. That left only one decision and you made it. I owe you a warm embrace for that, my friend. . . . .

How wonderful that you've made plans to visit us towards winter. You cannot possibly look forward to our reunion more than I, and that should give you some idea. Next letter will contain a few words from the children in their own hand. Many regards to Lien and Ben, all the children and kisses for you both from

Your Gait

Signs of Life

Notes

1. Albert Stibbe is Gerrit's nephew, the son of his oldest sister, Caroline.
2. Artis is the zoological garden in Amsterdam.
3. Nathan Dasberg was Gerrit's close friend, an orthodox Jew (as such he was prohibited from shaving) and leader of the Jewish community in Hilversum. After the war he emigrated to Israel with his wife, their five children, and a large number of Jewish orphans whom they adopted and raised as their own.
4. Holland refers to the central provinces of North and South Holland which had not yet been liberated.
5. Barend had sent a telegram to the City Hall in Heerenveen inquiring into "the whereabouts of Gerrit Verdoner." The population registry office had sent a standard reply regarding Barend's own departure from Heerenveen in 1910!

Extract from one of Gerrit's letters, describing some of his experiences while in hiding.

Hilversum, September 19, 1945

I was staying at the home of an evangelist in the Nieuwe Krim near Coevorden, and slept underneath the church for ten weeks. Next door was a grocer, a strict Calvinist, where you could find me every evening because a couple of very pleasant Jewish women were in hiding there. They baked real Jewish cake every Friday and saved the largest pieces for me. They also made soup almost every day, and since the evangelist's wife couldn't cook, let alone make soup, I would have a couple of delicious bowls of soup there *after* leaving my host's table. In short, they spoiled me rotten over there. Every evening we enjoyed ourselves enormously until 10:30, when in the pitch dark I would return to the church by a backway across the fields and crawl through a small trapdoor under the pulpit—and wind up underneath the church, where I would sleep *and sleep well!* on top of four potato sacks filled with straw. Sometimes the rats would visit me (God's truth), and then I would tell myself: better rats than Krauts, and sleep with the blankets pulled over my head in order to prevent them from chewing up my nose. I made a feeble attempt to combat this Egyptian plague with some rat poison, but was glad to be leaving there just the same (the "Gruenen" with their bloodhounds were taking up quarters nearby, and I didn't care for that at all).

My next stop was with three bachelor farmers who lived an hour down the road in the middle of Drente's "jungle." Cultivated heath, a small farmstead. That was quite a circus. Let me tell you about it. Three brothers, bachelors, as I noted; the youngest was forty-two, the oldest fifty-two; the mother was seventy-four. Two other people were hiding out there, two Russians, escaped prisoners of war. A dirty mess like you wouldn't believe. There was a single room with two bedsteads in the wall and a tiny alcove that could barely hold a regular-size bed. The farm woman slept in the one bedstead, two of the brothers in the other, and the third in the bed. In addition there was a small threshing-floor and a small barn. The threshing-floor held sacks of wheat, rye, etc. A large oven, and in the barn two cows, a horse, and two sheep. Outside in the sheds a few tools and an enormous pig weighing two hundred kilos. The Russians and myself slept in a chicken coop (which are as large as a small room in these parts), surrounded by bundles of straw and straw on the floor as well. We slept there like logs though the temperature was way below freezing. I spent four weeks there after which I again went to Friesland, in December 1944. There was no outhouse. You'd just squat down next to a tree with your bare behind exposed to the freezing cold. That room was never cleaned. Never. In the morning, the youngest Russian would sweep the floor and under the chests of drawers with a small brush as far as he could reach—and then the house was clean! But what GLUTTONY!! I must spell it out in capital letters or I wouldn't be doing justice to my worthy hosts. To begin with, they never delivered a single liter of milk to the Germans. That would be helping the enemy and they were deadset against that. They did their own churning and so had plenty of butter. They did not smoke, and all summer long traded their smoking coupons for butter, which they preserved in brine, and this gave them even more butter. So much milk you couldn't drink it all and oatmeal that was out of this world. Bread made only with their own wheat, whole-grain bread; a pig weighing two hundred kilos had been slaughtered the previous September, and I was given so much meat, sausage, and bacon at meals that I routinely passed along a part of my meat-filled plate to one of the Russians. Delicious potatoes, lots of vegetables, often jars of fruit they had preserved themselves—in short, a kind of hospitality that's hard to imagine. And they constantly kept urging me to eat more. On the roof they had a Windcharger (for electricity), and every evening we'd listen to the radio and carry on long discussions with these fellows, who were, I must say, quite up on things. And since they had turf from their own peat-bog, we never lacked for heat. When I wanted to leave for Friesland, they told me: "Uncle Gerrit, here you know what you've got, but you don't know what you may be getting over there; I would think it over if I were you." And although I had spent four weeks with them, they wouldn't accept as much as a dime. I stopped by there before I returned to [western] Holland [after the war] and you should have seen how they came running from the fields when they heard that it was me. And had I let them, they would have stuffed my car with everything they could manage to haul up to it. They were real GENTLEMEN, even if they never took a bath. I loved those fellows. And the reason they liked me so much was that they thought of me as a very important person who never put on any airs with them. But you know I couldn't have acted any differently.

We would always disappear into the barn whenever people visited, which was seldom, and you could see whoever was coming within a radius of five hundred meters and even further. So no one knew that we were there—at least that's what we thought! But as far as I was concerned it was still too close to the border and I reasoned, the border being so close, here is where the Germans will make a stand. And indeed, more and more "Gruenen" started showing up in

Signs of Life

the area. As I had already written to Friesland, they [the underground] came to get me right away. This had to be done by bicycle, seventy-five kilometers, and to think that in fifteen months all I had moved were my eyelids (for sleeping) and my jaws; but as far as any physical exercise worthy of the name, forget it. Somehow I did complete those seventy-five kilometers, but don't ask how I managed to get down from the bicycle. I had to lift the one leg over the frame with my two hands.

After I had been gone for two weeks, they were tipped off that there would be a search. So they dug a hole on the heath and that's where the two Russians slept. And wouldn't you know, a week later a bunch of policemen, Dutch Nazis, accompanied by Germans paid them a visit at night and searched everything. But the chicken coop was empty; nor did they discover that hole on the heath. The Russians slept there until the liberation in April, and by that time I had long been sleeping in a marvelous huge double bed in Oranjewoud—with breakfast in bed, including an egg, at eight o'clock. That woman's pea soup was something I will not easily forget; it was even better than at home. But then they had slaughtered two pigs (one "legal" and one "illegal") and into the soup went a two-liter canning-jar filled with porkmeat. From a material point of view, it was "phénoménal," to use René's expression, and except for occasional tension and restlessness, I was free. That must be why I also remained in good shape mentally. Besides, at the time I still thought that we would see our parents and Hil again. It probably was a good thing that I didn't know anything more, for if I had I wouldn't have come out as well as I did.

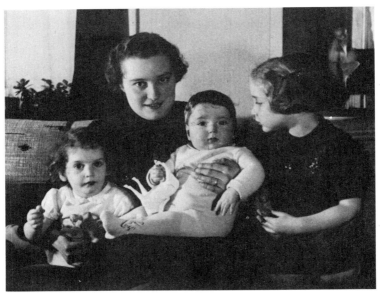

Frans, Otto, and Yoka with Grada Smits, 1939.

Hilde with Yoka, Otto, and Frans, 1942, just before the family separated to go into hiding. Many Jewish families had photographs like this taken before going into hiding.

Signs of Life

Otto in the garden of the Hopperus Buma family home in Diepenveen.

Yoka at the baptism of Roosje Rijnders, Woubrugge, December 1943.

Frans at the children's zoo (Artis), Amsterdam, 1944.

Signs of Life

HILDE'S LETTERS
TO GRADA
1942

*Grada watches Yoka feed the greengrocer's
horse in our driveway, 1939.*

Introduction
To Letters To Grada

Grada Smits, to whom this and the subsequent letter is addressed, had taken care of the three Verdoner children from 1935 to 1941. Since she was not Jewish she was less affected by the German occupation. Grada started work as a part-time mother's helper when she was seventeen years old and Yoka was an infant. Two years later, when Fran was expected, Grada was working full time. By the time Otto was born, she was living in. She worked for us until 1941 when she became engaged to Hans van de Beek, whom she married in 1942. The friendship between Grada and our family extended to many other family members. "Mr. and Mrs. Wallman," mentioned in this letter, were Hilde's much loved aunt and uncle, Paul and Selma, who lived nearby in Hilversum. Selma was the sister of Hilde's mother.

The first letter to "Nanny," as we called her, and her future husband, Hans, was written by Hilde after the German occupation was in full operation in The Netherlands, but while the family was still together. There was not yet any talk of sending the children into hiding, although by the time the

1942   85

second letter was written, just a few months later, that idea was already developing. In March of 1942, Hilde was struggling to cope with each new restriction individually and also trying to deal with everyday life. Yoka had to attend a school on the other side of town because it was the only Jewish school in the area. Although she would not ordinarily have been sent to a Jewish school, the Nazis had already barred Jews from Dutch schools so there was no choice. Fran, who was in kindergarten, stayed there because of the courage of the kindergarten teacher, Miss Dierkens, who refused to comply with the German regulations. However, school ended suddenly when the family was forced to move to Amsterdam.

Hilde's allusion to Gerrit's business, "The business is gone altogether," seems very matter of fact in writing. However, the loss of the business due to Nazi confiscation of all Jewish businesses caused the family much anger and fear.

In spite of all these problems, Hilde is still hoping to go to Grada and Hans' wedding if it is not too far away. A Nazi ruling no longer permitted Jews to ride on trains, and Hilde and Gerrit would certainly not have risked a train ride to The Hague to attend the wedding. The Germans routinely checked the identity papers of passengers.

The postscript after the signature in the first letter refers to Toos Venema, another young woman who worked in the household. When the family was forced to move to Amsterdam—an event which occurred between the first and second letters—Toos came along for a short time. However, it was forbidden for her, as a gentile, to work for Jews and she soon left. After the war, when Gerrit and his children moved back to Hilversum, Toos and her husband and small daughter moved in with them to keep house.

Both these letters are signed Hilde Verdoner-Sluizer. This follows Dutch usage for names of married women: first name, married name, maiden name.

Grada and Hans contributed the two letters which follow, as well as the one written from Westerbork which appears later on in the text. These two letters are included even though they were not written from Westerbork because they show how Nazism increasingly restricted the family's movements and controlled the minutest details of everyday life.

In 1987, after forty-five years, Fran visited Grada and Hans. It was an emotional reunion. Grada said she hadn't believed she would ever see Fran again; she didn't know whether to laugh or cry from excitement. She related how much she had learned from our mother, especially about taking care of babies. Hans showed off his prize-winning fuchsia collection, and they had a lovely dinner. After dinner Grada mentioned that they still had the baby bed that they had borrowed from our family. "Wouldn't you like to have it back? You know, we only borrowed it! We kept it for you; you may have it any time if you can find a way to ship it." It was amazing that such a thing still existed after so many years. They all climbed to the attic, and there was a beautiful little wooden bed painted white with pink trim. Hans and Grada's two sons and five grandchildren had made fine use of it, they said, and it had traveled with them as far away as Indonesia (at that time the Dutch East Indies) where Hans had been sent as a military officer. Hans confessed that he had had to repaint the crib several times, but he had been careful always to use the same colors! And then Grada told the following remarkable story:

In 1942 Otto, then three years old, went to an orphanage while our parents searched for a more permanent situation for him. It was not a Jewish orphanage but there were Jewish children there. As the orphanage did not have enough beds, children were asked to bring their own; Otto was sent with this crib. As a baby, Otto had the habit of crawling under the blankets to the foot of the bed to sleep against the footboard, completely covered by the bedding. One day there was a raid on the orphanage; the Gestapo was always well informed and knew exactly who the Jewish children were. While the Gestapo was going through the dormitory the director of the orphanage noticed that Otto had, as usual, crawled to the base of his bed and she quickly turned back the sheet and the blanket as if the bed was empty and airing.

By her quick thinking and action, Otto was passed over and saved.

Today this crib is in Fran's house. Hilde's great grand-daughter, Rachel Jeanne, sleeps in it when she visits.

Hilversum, March 25, 1942

Dear Nanny and Hans,

We were very happy to get your cheerful letter, and I am very sorry that it took me such a long time to answer it.

In particular I had wanted to send you our very best wishes in time to reach you before the publication of your banns, but even though that happy day was a week ago, I hope that you will realize that our best wishes for happiness and prosperity in your future life together are no less warm or sincere for being late, and we hope that you may have a liberal share of happiness and prosperity in a bright future. The very fact that it takes so much more effort to really and truly enjoy your budding happiness in these cheerless times will cause it to flower and grow ever so much more beautifully; and the best thing I could wish for you is that some time—and we all hope that will be very soon—when the sun shines again on our cozy homes, your inner sun will far out-shine it, for that sun within is at all times still the greatest and most wonderful source of warmth and light.

Since I think I know you both fairly well, especially you, dear Nanny, (it will always be Nanny, even if you have a slew of children of your own one day!) for you were after all a member of my family for several years, I feel certain that you have what it takes to face the future with confidence. I am sure that you two will make each other happy and will make a good home together.

The children cheered when they heard Nanny was getting married, and the prospect of staying over at Nanny and Hans' is of course the greatest bliss imaginable.

　　　　　　　　　　　　　　　　　　　　　Signs of Life

Where will the wedding take place? If it is going to be in The Hague, we probably won't be able to attend for logistical reasons, but if it should be in Hollandsche Rading, we'll manage to get there somehow.

I imagine it is quite a job to collect everything that is needed for your household, even though you had managed to accumulate quite a few things over the past few years. Have you found a house yet, or will you rent a furnished place for the time being, the way so many young people do now that houses are so hard to come by? Of course you are still going to get a wedding gift from us. I just put off buying a gift because I first wanted to ask you if there is anything in particular that you still need for your household, for I would like to fulfill a special wish, as far as that is possible these days, with the very limited selection in the shops. With my practical bent I would greatly enjoy giving you something that you can really use, so please send me a wish list soon, dear Nanny.

Although I realize that you are terribly busy just now, we would all very much enjoy having you two visit us again some time during the next few weeks. Are you coming this way for the Easter holidays by any chance? Just let us know ahead of time if and when you are coming.

Belatedly, many thanks for your good wishes on the occasion of Fransje's birthday. Frankie herself was thrilled with the lovely card she received from you. Your earlier birthday letter for Yoka also arrived promptly, and I also have it lying in front of me right here. I have to admit that I had intended to reply in detail, but never got beyond the good intentions; you know how it is with my writing. But once I start, there is no stopping the flow of words, for I really enjoy telling you all about us again. The more so because I know how much it interests you.

But during those endless cold and dark winter days there is too little time to go around anyway, so that writing gets put off again and again. Now, with the return of spring and warm sunshine, energy sprouts again. For the first time this year, the children were able to play in the yard again all day yesterday and today, and soft spring air flowed into the house through all the open windows.

Yoka now attends a school at the Utrechtseweg near the Berkenlaan; you know how terribly far that is, but it is the only Jewish school, so there was nothing we could do about it. She is very happy there, however, and likes it very much, and she enjoys being allowed to take the bus from the station to go there all by herself. So you see that this problem which caused us much worry and grief does not disturb her one bit.

Frankie is still with Miss Dierkens, who simply will not let go of her, so we are just leaving it at that for the time being. Otje stays home, of course, and busies himself with pushing his wheelbarrow around the yard. He can ride the little tricycle now, and he is having a good time dragging his cars and animals around. All three of them have grown a good bit, fortunately, and have gotten through the cold winter well, knock on wood!!

Yoka is big enough now so that I could even take some lovely skating trips with her, and last summer she had to get a bigger bike. All those things happen so gradually, and yet so very fast!

Mr. Verdoner is also doing well, but the business is gone altogether! Several weeks ago the rumor went around all of a sudden that all Jews would have to leave the area. You will understand what an awful prospect that was for us, and we were trying to take all sorts of precautionary measures. It looks as if the danger is over for the moment, but of course things can change again any minute. Mr. and Mrs. Wallman also still live in the same house, but like us, they were very miserable too because of the threat of evacuation, as it is called nowadays, no doubt to give it an air of dignity.

Perhaps those rumors have reached your area too, or Hans may have heard something or other about it. Perhaps I'll tell you more about this at some other time, if we get a chance.

We have recovered from the shock by now, little by little, and at home our lives have more or less returned to normal. That is above all why I could not immediately reply to your letter last week.

Doesn't Jeanne have any wedding plans yet? Or won't they let her go yet at De Lange's? I was surprised to hear that there is another baby on the way, but I am happy for her anyway; you know how I feel about babies! Are your parents well? And how is Leidie? I haven't seen her anymore after last summer either.

Well, dear Nanny and Hans, this letter was a long time in coming, but I hope that you now have some idea again of how we are doing. As you can tell, we are doing all right considering the circumstances, and as long as we can stay in our home and be left in peace we'll be quite content for the time being.

I hope that you will soon find the time to drop us a line, dear Nanny, and especially don't forget the wish list. Please tell us something about your future plans, for you know I am deeply interested, even though I may take a long time again to reply.

Once more, very best wishes in all respects for the two of you, and kindest regards also from my husband, and kisses from the children. Hope to see you soon.

Yours very sincerely,
Hilde Verdoner-Sluizer

Toos sends her best regards too and best wishes. She will probably write you soon.

Amsterdam, July 6, 1942

Dear Nanny and Hans,

Now your honeymoon is almost over, so I dare to intrude with a letter in reply to your cheerful, loving letter, dear Nanny, which we were so terribly happy to have. You have no idea how very happy we were to get such a truly loving letter, especially now in these terribly dismal times. I was pleased to read that you have made such good progress on your home and I think I can tell from the tone of your letter that you have not yet smashed all your plates over each other's heads. That would not be possible, anyway, in these days when even plates are rationed.

Of course I would love to take a peek at your place, but I am afraid I'll have to have a little patience, for traveling is now so difficult for me that I only do it in the greatest emergencies.

The children would love to spend the night at Nanny and Hans' house no doubt, but I don't know if I should burden you with that just yet: such an intrusion in your new little nest. This week Fransje is going to spend a few days with Toos, who will be picking her up on Thursday. Of course Frankie is eagerly looking forward to the event, and it may also bring some color to her cheeks, which she could use. Yoka's vacation starts this coming Friday, and I trust she will come home with a good final report card. Then she may go and stay with you of course; I am sure that will be a lovely and unexpected reward.

I have a proposition to make, namely, could the two of you possibly come and visit us one of these days? Or if you cannot come together, perhaps Hans would give Nanny a day off? We could talk things over then, and you might even take Yoka back with you right then. It goes without saying that I would take care of the travel expenses.

Will you please let me know if and when the two of you, or one of you, will be with us, perhaps in the course of this week? I'll have to say good-bye for now, and hope to have the chance to hear all your news in person soon. All of us here send our kindest regards, and a hug from each of the children.

Warmest regards and very best wishes,

H. Verdoner-Sluizer

Gerrit's parents, Henriette and Abraham Verdoner.

Hilde with her parents, David and Bertha Sluizer.

Paul and Selma Wallman with their daughter, Charlotte.

LETTERS FROM WESTERBORK JANUARY TO APRIL 1943

Hilde and Gerrit on their wedding day, 1933.

Introduction
To Hilde's Letters
January To April 1943

Hilde's first letter from Westerbork, written about a month after she first arrived there on December 18, 1942, reveals the many layers of her existence—her complex relationship with Gerrit; her worries about her three children, all in hiding now; and her concern for coping as best she could in the camp.

Gerrit and Hilde had gotten married in 1933, when Hilde was twenty-four and Gerrit thirty-four. Gerrit had been a popular bachelor who had taken a long time to settle down, and apparently there had been conflicts and difficulties in the marriage. Gerrit liked delicious meals; Hilde hated to cook. Gerrit liked being on time; Hilde thought nothing of being late. Gerrit had been the darling of a doting mother and three sisters, not to mention many girlfriends; Hilde was matter of fact and down to earth. Both Gerrit and Hilde were devoted parents who loved having children, but the marriage had gotten a bit frayed around the edges at the time world events engulfed the family. The tensions of the times no doubt exacerbated these underlying stresses.

The children, too, experienced the rising tension in the household. One day Yoka came home from school to find Hilde on a stepladder taking down the curtains in an already bare living room, because the Germans had commandeered all the homes on our street. Yoka proudly told about a new song they had learned in her first grade class that day, "Holland, My Holland," and was puzzled and upset when Hilde reacted to this information with anger and bitterness. There were quarrels between Gerrit and Hilde, and much unhappiness as the family tried to deal with each new and threatening situation.

This is the background of the opening passage of Hilde's first letter. Apparently Gerrit had been very much angered by something that had happened. It is not clear to us what had made Gerrit so angry because we do not have his letters, but it may have been Hilde's attempt to buy a false identity card for him, without informing him first, from a man who proved to be an undercover Nazi agent. As a result Hilde was arrested as she left this meeting. Hilde writes, "It is impossible to say at this time whether what I did was right or wrong," a sentiment which applies not only to this incident, but to many of the life-or-death decisions men and women were forced to make at that time, in total ignorance of the underlying reality. Hilde's response to Gerrit's anger reveals her thoughts, hopes, and fears about their marriage. It is also clear from her letters that the bond between Gerrit and Hilde was strong in spite of their differences.

In her letters, Hilde refers to her three children as "trio," the name Gerrit and Hilde had always used for us, but here the euphemism is intentional, as are many other circumlocutions. References to health or illness, for example, are usually code for someone's safety or danger. Thus, when Hilde asks what the outcome was of the contagious disease in Yoka's neighborhood, she is referring to the raid that had taken place on the children's home in Zeist, Yoka's first hiding place. The outcome, incidentally, was that many of the Jewish children who remained there were deported, together with the two middle-aged ladies who ran the home. Yoka had been removed before this raid took place and thus escaped deportation.

Yoka, seven years old at the time, clearly remembers the day Hilde took her to the home in Zeist, installing her there with some of her own things—a bookshelf and a cyclamen plant—and then leaving. Even then she knew who some of the other Jewish children were. Hilde occasionally managed to visit, bicycling through the woods, since she could no longer use public transportation. Hilde's visit on November 16, 1942, Yoka's eighth birthday, turned out to be the last time they ever saw each other, as Hilde was arrested shortly afterwards and sent to Westerbork.

Hilde found life in Westerbork "quite bearable" at first because initially she was the only one of her family to be there. She had "only myself to take care of," and she had "good hopes that at least a large part of our family . . .may remain in good health"; that is, she hoped a large part of the family would stay out of the clutches of the Germans. Of all the immediate family, only Hilde's youngest brother, Otto, was in Westerbork at this time. Hilde also found life in Westerbork bearable at first because she was surrounded by many Jewish friends and relatives. Ironically, life was much simpler once one was in the camp and no longer had to live in constant fear of raids and imminent arrest. Amsterdam, to her and many other Jews at the time, was "a paved nightmare."

In the camp Hilde was very busy. Inmates had jobs, and some of these jobs also gave the illusion of safety from deportation. After work, Hilde rushed about, visiting sick relatives in the hospital; "organizing" food, that is, trying to obtain it by means of pilfering or barter of one kind or another; trying to relay messages, arrange contacts, write letters, and take care of all the necessities for surviving in the camp. Hilde appears to have been very resourceful in these activities.

All of Hilde's letters written between January and April 1943, during her first stay in Westerbork, are typewritten because Hilde had a job as secretary in the camp administration and thus had access to a typewriter. Emissaries from the Jewish Council who visited the camp regularly on official business probably smuggled these letters out, since inmates, as Hilde mentions, officially were allowed to write only one twelve-line letter every three weeks. Hilde warns Gerrit never to refer to her letters when he writes to her, since incoming mail was carefully censored.

Trains left Westerbork almost every Tuesday from July 15, 1942, until September 3, 1944. Every train carried approximately one thousand Jews to concentration and extermination camps in Poland, Germany, and Czechoslovakia. In all, ninety-three such trains left Westerbork. Although camp inmates did not know exactly what awaited them in "the East," everyone's desperate efforts were bent on not going on transport, but staying in Westerbork and on Dutch soil as long as possible. Thus much of Hilde's letters, too, deals with her efforts to obtain the "right" papers for herself and others, and her despair when more friends and relatives had been deported. Around March 22, Hilde writes, "Last Friday, we ceremoniously celebrated our three months' anniversary here. Of our group of about eighty people, only a very few are left, no more than about ten."

By April 1943, the tone of the letters grows less cheerful and more anxious. In an undated letter to Gerrit, probably written at this time, Hilde emphatically urges him to tell her Aunt Selma and Uncle Paul, German refugees in their sixties who had not yet been arrested, that they must sleep upstairs and not on the ground floor, since their chances of escaping or of avoiding being found are better if they are further away from the front door. On April 12, Hilde writes that her Aunt Kee has been deported, "but it was a hopeless case which could not be helped." While she is in the middle of writing this letter, news reaches her that Paul and Selma have indeed been arrested, "which made me feel as if I had been hit over the head with a heavy club."

In June 1943, Hilde was released from Westerbork as a result of Gerrit's job with the Jewish Council, although her freedom proved to be temporary. This is where the first series of her letters ends.

[Mid January 1943]

Dear Gerrit,

Now that I finally have managed to free an hour for myself and have received permission from dear Mrs. Neuburger to use her private palace for a while in pursuit of this project, I want to write this, my first type-written letter from here, to you.

I am now at the point where I am getting over the terrible blow I received between Christmas and New Year's; a blow softened by time, weeks full of eventful days having passed in the meanwhile, which do not leave one time to reflect on one's own petty little miseries; it was blotted out, finally, by the many loving letters which I received from you since then.

Of course it was clear to me at once that for some reason or other you had reached your limit once again, but that it would get to the point where you would vent all your anger on me in writing, and with such vehemence, was the most miserable experience I have ever had or ever hope to have in my life. After all, it is really not my fault that everybody has been telling you how brave I am—I trust that you will believe me when I say that I did not ask anybody to tell you that. If anything, I gave visiting friends the message for you not to worry about me, just to reassure you that I was all right. For me, the die had been cast, and I was determined to get through all this the best I could. I was, and still am, thankful every day that no others have come to harm through my actions, and I am sure that a lot of the credit for that goes to you as well.

It is impossible to say at this time whether what I did was right or wrong, so it is useless to worry about it. In any case, I believe that everything had already been arranged for the trio as well as possible, at least for the first six months. By the way, what was the outcome of the contagious disease in Yoka's neighborhood? Did the other children who were with her there also move in the meantime? You've written so little about these things and I haven't heard anything from Grada yet. Did you find the inventory list which was meant for her? The remainder of the money may be sent to Otto who is paid up until my mother's birthday. As you can see, I am slipping into the practical messages. I kindly request that you answer these as fully as possible. There are still many unanswered questions from my last letter too. I mean the letter I wrote prior to my trip of December 18.

It is probably true that my letters are full of instructions, but I don't think that many of these are for my own benefit, for I find myself very unimportant, believe me, and I would manage quite well on my own resources if only I might be assured that everything I ought to be doing for others will continue to be done in spite of my absence. Please do not think that out of sight means out of mind where you are concerned either, because, even if I am not darning your socks and cooking your food (things which anyone else can do for you as well as I, or better) all my efforts were directed towards the goal of being reunited with you in good health whenever peace may come again. With my feminine shortsightedness I may have made the wrong decision, but really, greater minds than yours or mine have made similar and even worse mistakes. If I asked you to pick out sheets and towels for Toos, the reason was that I had promised her these things, so why shouldn't I, especially since I know that you don't begrudge her a thing either, and that she has always done her utmost to be helpful

Signs of Life

to us in every way. It is true that I may view life in a simplis-
tic way and you may be right in saying that I lack imagina-
tion. Nor is it my style to say sweet things; I want to show
my feelings for people through my actions. The fact that
you always thought you got the short end of the stick in this
respect may have been well-founded at times, especially
during the last few years (and not only since my absence of
the last six months). I know that it was becoming too difficult for me to battle the torrents of your dissatisfaction
with me. However hard I tried to do things right, they always turned out wrong. I tried often enough to talk to you
about it, but the words would never flow, and I finally gave
up trying. Please don't make a bigger thing out of it than it
really is and don't look for any hidden meanings, because
the only meaning is that I wished so fervently for everything to be one hundred percent right between us, or at
least as close to one hundred percent as we could get, for
you know how much I like things to be as good and as clear
as possible. Please do not think that I believe that I could
have made a happier life married to someone else. It is just
that I am so sorry to have failed to take better advantage of
my, of our, opportunities. My defect is that I don't have it
in me, and what you don't have in you, you cannot give out.
It is too bad that you are the victim of this defect, since you
happen to be married to me. Perhaps you would have been
much happier with another wife. After all the thinking I
have done over the past few years, I have come to the conclusion that there is no man I would rather have been married to, since with you I've probably made the best I could
have of marriage and family, considering my inadequacies.
It is quite possible that you do not think the results very
worthwhile, but I am at peace with them and I have accepted the fact that I am too stupid, too unimaginative, too
headstrong, and too unaffectionate to do any better.

Of course you have your faults too, like everybody
else, and you are quite aware of that yourself. My faults as
well as yours only became apparent in the course of time,

for one does not know one another's faults (or merits, for that matter) on one's wedding day. But I took you as you are, sparing myself the trouble of trying to change a man over thirty. I think, however, that you were bothered, and even angered, more and more by my faults. Thus, they became more and more prominent in your eyes, which naturally affected me; it is even possible that my faults did indeed become more prominent, things such as as my slow tempo and my lack of interest in cooking, to give a few examples. In the end I was so totally convinced that there was no pleasing you anymore, that perhaps my feelings for you, which really and truly also encompass a very deep affection, began to wane a bit. What a totally rotten time this is for all these explanations and, worse yet, by letter.

I send this letter off in fear and trepidation, because I shudder at the thought that you will once more interpret what I have written differently from the way it is intended. For your reply to my last postcard shows again that you misinterpreted several things I said. With "more victims" I meant my father, with whom you were so very curt that time when he came to see you at the Lijnbaansgracht[1] around Christmas. I was greatly bothered by the fact that this good man, in addition to all his other worries, was raked over the coals by you, for I know how much he suffers when you and I are having another of our stormy episodes, and under the present circumstances it is much worse. When I wrote you, "In any case, I wish you all the best," it was not meant as a farewell, just a goodbye, penned without any ulterior motives.

I know that at this time you are all having miserable days and especially evenings again, but really, prepare for the worst—that is the lesson I have learned in the meantime—and then decide to make the best of it. In the worst case, if you should be picked up after all, do take all your luggage right away and don't let yourself be talked into leaving it, with the assurance that you will be back shortly or that the luggage will be sent for later, because

Signs of Life

that never happens. If you should be questioned about me, stick to what was arranged with Martin Bloch: that may give you a better chance to be released. Please remember always that I have your welfare at heart, even if you might be tempted to conclude otherwise from my actions. But also try, if you can, not to be so irritated by my shortcomings which cannot be changed anyway. Otherwise there is no hope for us as a couple.

Life is quite bearable for me here, especially because I have only myself to take care of and because I am healthy and have good hopes that at least a large part of our family, and Jo, Lien, and Suze in addition, may remain in good health. There are only a few people here in such a favorable situation, and if they fall ill and become bedridden in the turmoil of two hundred people, body and spirit are sorely taxed. Life in the [unreadable] barracks requires a great deal of patience and flexibility from the healthy, too, and since most people do not possess these qualities, especially under this enormous pressure, explosions occur often.

In the daytime I fortunately spend very little time in the barrack, since I have my work, as most people here do. During meals it is always terribly noisy, and heavy battles are fought for the use of the stove by people wishing to heat food. The explicit language used during these battles could certainly have provided Heyermans with inspiration for several stories. In the evening people retire fairly quietly, depending on whether many or few new guests have arrived. The time between six-thirty and nine a.m. brings the din of doomsday, what with people getting up and having breakfast, until everybody has left for work.

I sleep very well here, as I did at home, but I am dead tired at night, not from my work, where I never rush, but from the incessant noise and movement of people around me all day long.

I have the top bunk of three, which in my opinion has many advantages—for those who are able to get into and out of one, that is. You have some space above, so that you

can move around on your bed; you don't have anyone toss-
ing about above you, and you have some storage space for
your stuff on the rafters. Consequently, my shoes are arranged up there; at night my clothes flutter from there; and
at the very top I managed to attach a clothes hanger which
holds my red dress and either my raincoat or my green over-
coat. There is also a nail somewhere on which to hang my
towel and washcloth. Everything else stays in the backpack
and the knapsack which, together with my folded blankets,
lie on my bed in the daytime and are put somewhere on a
bench or table at night when I make my bed.

As you can see, my life has been greatly simplified, and
only by convincing myself that this is some sort of very pe-
culiar ski vacation, can I keep the cheerful disposition
which people sometimes marvel at around here. Of course
it is also very pleasant that so many of our good friends and
relatives are here, and since we are relieved of a certain category of worries, you rarely see any really worried faces
around, especially among the people who have found useful employment here.

I see Dorus almost daily, he is one of the VIPs here and
when I am taking a stroll with him, hardly anyone passes
who does not greet him. All the people from Hilversum
who left a year ago are in managerial positions now and are
really very kind to Otto and myself.

I also see Rudi and Finy[2] almost every day. Rudi is
much appreciated here, as always, because he does such
good work and takes pleasure in doing it. Since he is the one
to receive the parcels, I always get mine delivered promptly.
But it is too bad that Ineke and Peter have been ailing, we
hope that they are finally on the mend.

Floortje Kool occupies the bunk next to mine; she's the
daughter of Kool from Tel Aviv—isn't that a coincidence! I
really enjoy having her next to me, because she's such a nice
person and very good company. Fortunately she got a good
position with the Jewish Council, so it is fairly likely that
she too will be able to stay here for now. As it happens,

there is much ado here today, since a great many changes are expected and no one knows exactly what they will be. What eventually will remain of this camp, whether part of it will be moved to Vught[3], no one knows; perhaps the future will be a little more clear in a week.

This afternoon, Bl. sent for me: his sending for me was quite an honor in itself. He was in a great hurry, as usual, but extremely friendly all the same, and he gave me your best regards. It is possible that he knows more about the things to come, but if he does, he certainly doesn't tell me about it. I dare not approach our former neighbor, Blum's guest, or Schles., at all just now, for there is trouble in the air. However, they always treat me in the most friendly manner.

Perhaps my writing is a bit disjointed: the reason is that I have moved my typewriter to Dorus' barrack in the meantime and the place is teeming with people coming and going, men and women cooking and eating all around me.

How are all of you doing in the meantime? Please write more extensively about all the subjects that would interest me.

I was given Lé's best regards the other day and I was very happy to have some news of him that way. It does make a difference, getting a personal message like that and being told in person how things are going.

Of course I talk to Mie and Hartog every day—they are really doing quite well, given the circumstances. There is no chance of their being admitted to the hospital, however, because fortunately (or in this case unfortunately, actually!) their physical condition is such that they are not eligible for hospitalization. I am still trying to have him placed as a sanitary worker in Quarantine, but it seems all but impossible. Dorus, being a dyed-in-the-wool camp inmate, is assisting me in this thing, too.

Among the many old friends living here are Willy Kan with Suzy and the children, who have been here for several months. They all look quite well, as do most of our friends, who receive care packages regularly.

Now I have to mention some practical matters. In the first place, I would like you to have the laundry which I shipped you yesterday, washed as soon as possible. Unfortunately my woolen stockings have holes in them and since I have no wool here, perhaps Aunt Selma or otherwise your mother may be willing to mend them for me. The pillowcase is also worn out, so please send me another one next time.

I would also like to have my blue shoes to wear in the overshoes. After I receive those I shall return another pair for repair. Also, I'd like the other writing pad, the large, lined one; it should be in the brown leather (accordion) suitcase. And a few notebooks (lined). Yoka may need some of these too, come to think of it. I am almost out of toilet soap, there is plenty more in the closet. I would also like the green woolen polo shirt from the same closet. Also a jar of marmite to use on my bread. If Fransje needs larger shoes, Corrie v. Abs has them.

Speaking of shoes, I would like to ask you if you could possibly find a pair of rubber overshoes size 11 for my barrack leader. It would really be important for me to do him a favor with such galoshes, but I don't want you to give him yours. Perhaps you know someone who wants to sell a pair. It would really be a good deed, because it is impossible to get around here in regular shoes. I haven't worn the riding boots yet, I usually wear my ski boots, but they are not totally waterproof either.

Mother's little pan is quite useful and the contents were utterly delicious. I am not very much in need of hot food, however. Of course whatever is sent tastes better than camp food, but it is such a struggle to get it warmed up and if you use canned heat it takes so much fuel. I would, however, appreciate some roast beef and perhaps a jar of pickles every now and then, and apples!!!! And finally, please include toilet paper regularly.

Of course I do not want to tempt fate by mentioning your continuing good luck, and Bl. just this afternoon assured me that he will try to hold on to you indefinitely, but I would advise you to consider making alternative arrangements with Rob's mother and with Wim S. for the sending of care packages.

What news do you have from Karl and Hans Br[andt]?[4] Is everything still as before with them and do they expect it to stay that way? I am so glad you ordered calcium for Mrs. N. That reminds me: my Calfortan has to be refilled, too, so please include a large bottle. I know I am making a million requests, and I only hope that you will not be too overburdened with them! Now who would you say is in the more enviable position, you who have to run a thousand errands for me, or I, who get the benefit of your help? I am beginning to think that this is about the worst letter I have ever written, but I find it impossible to collect my thoughts here; moreover, I have so many things to tell you and to ask you that I don't know where to start.

Please write me often, your letters give me such great pleasure, although they are threatening to impose restrictions on incoming mail. At any rate, it is quite difficult for me to reply. I cannot write at night, as the lights are turned off at ten, and I rarely if ever have the opportunity in the daytime. Sending the letters is a big problem, too, which I don't think you understand, judging by your repeated requests for replies.

[Hand-written continuation at the bottom]

Officially, just the *one* 12-line letter is allowed every three weeks. I would really also like some rye bread at some time. Actually, I am ashamed of all these food requests, because this way I have more food here than I would have if I were at home. Is it difficult to arrange all this? I had a case of apples on order from Corrie v. A. From that order, parcels could be sent regularly, if you were to arrange this with

Rob, and all of you could also get some of them. Just received a letter from Karl and Hans. I would be very pleased if he came here and I would like to know exactly when he will be coming.

Dear Gerrit,

On rereading this letter, I thought it turned out to be such a lousy one, all in all, that I would prefer not to send it. However, since I did not want to leave you without news any longer, and since it may be a long time before I can write you a better letter, you'll have to take it as it is. I do hope you are well, and that you will have the good sense to go on as best you can, even though it may be very difficult for you. That, after all, is the only way we have a chance of surviving. Take good care of your health and stay calm. Spend as much time as possible with friends, either in the van Breestraat or at Fen and Jan's. Also around the Pretorius[straat]⁵ where we have so many good friends.

Don't dwell on how beautiful and pleasant life could have been, because one always tends to idealize things and we have to get through this anyway. Also, please don't think that I do not sympathize with your problems, but on the larger scale of things they are so insignificant and you really have to have the conviction that the strength to survive all this has to come from within and that no one, not even the most ideal spouse or anyone else, can help you if you do not also muster all your own strength.

I shall try to write you again soon and, if possible, tell you a bit more about my daily activities here. I am doing well, and most importantly, I am healthy and always busy at work. Last week's cold spell had the great advantage that we had no mud for a couple of days. After the thaw, the mud was virtually impossible to trudge through. As you can see, everything has its advantages and disadvantages, here as everywhere.

Lots of love and kisses from
Hilde

[By hand in the margins]

Be sure to read everything I wrote in the other margins carefully.

Please be sure to give my best regards to Bé[6], also from Otto, and many thanks for the delicious truffles she sent. My father's letters are always very pleasant and I shall try to write him soon. Please tell him that Chaya Oldstein [?] sends her best regards and thanks for the good [illegible]. Also, Gerzon [?], Uncle Frits Hirsch's administrator [?] sends his regards to Father—we eat at the same table. The pickles Otto received from Father and Mother were delicious!

Yesterday I went to the hairdresser to have my hair washed and waved, such luxury! They did an excellent job. While I was there, one of the police officers came for a haircut. Please also send one or more parcels as [illegible] or a bottle of liquid Supercrème [?] from suitcase with the others. Also please the blue jar of cream and the powder from vanity.

Please try your very best to get the rubber boots size 11. Perhaps you know someone who will *not* need them for a while and is willing to sell them secondhand. Could you also locate a ski suit for Lotte Heider?

If you hear any more about Vught, please write me. We are all in the dark about that here. Otto lives with a very congenial group of *halutzim*[7], excellent morale. I am in quite pleasant company, too, with many people I got to know at the Schouwburg and with whom I have gradually become good friends, under these circumstances.

Just received the tablets for Mrs. Neub. This evening, I am going to a meeting of *halutzim* with Otto. I hope I have not written anything that is unpleasant or bothersome to you! If only I were a bit more dependent on you, that would be [illegible] better!

Remember *never* to refer to my letter in your reply. Apparently, they are censoring more heavily now, and the rumor is that restrictions will be imposed on the sending of packages. It is impossible to write a letter here that is better than the most [illegible] of all letters. Your shipments are always marvelous, and I wonder how you manage to get hold of everything. Please also some [illegible] such as Patria, just one if need be. [illegible] as soon as possible.

Lots of love and kisses,
Hilde

Notes

1. Lijnbaansgracht 366 is the address of one of the offices of the Jewish Council where Gerrit was employed.
2. Rudi Gersons was Hilde's cousin; Finy was his wife.
3. Vught was a concentration camp in Brabant, a province in the south of the Netherlands.
4. Karl and Hans Brandt were neighbors in Hilversum. Karl was German, not Jewish; his wife, Hans, was Jewish. They were very helpful in many ways. On one occasion Karl took Otto, three years old, to a safer address in another town, traveling by bicycle with Otto on the back.
5. Pretoriusstraat 89, in the Amsterdam ghetto established by the Nazis, was where Hilde's parents were living at the time, having been forced to move there from their home.
6. Bé Pimentel was a family friend who was engaged to Otto at one time.
7. *Halutzim* is a Hebrew word meaning pioneers. This was a Zionist organization which prepared young people to immigrate to Palestine and work in agriculture.

February 11, 1943

My Dear Gerrit,

Since tomorrow will be letter day again, I am taking advantage of a free moment to start a chat with you: otherwise this letter might not be finished by the time it has to be handed in tomorrow.

I am happy to report that your wonderful long letter from the Lijnbaan arrived last week at long last, together with your note and the photocopies regarding Nette[1]. As it happens, there is no need for these anymore, as Nette received her [exemption] stamp in the meantime.

It had been a very long time since I last heard from you! I understand that you cannot always find the time to write me long letters, what with the many worries that are constantly on your mind, but if I had my way, I'd have a little note from you every single day! On the other hand, that would make me feel even worse about not being able to reply more often.

You cannot imagine how time flies here: by the time I've finished my work, there is hardly any evening left. No sooner have we finished dinner than it is time to turn in for the night. The lights are turned off without fail; there isn't a minute's reprieve, not even for me, although I have managed to gain a certain amount of notoriety with the barrack leaders for always being the last one out of the washroom.

Fortunately, I still have the pleasure of having Floortje Kool in the bunk next to mine. We get along extremely well, and consequently spend a lot of time in long, animated conversations. From time to time we feast together on a cracker with butter and jam—better than the best pastries! It is such a joy to be working in the same office with her. It means we have the same working hours, often get to eat meals together, and in the evenings trudge through the darkness together to the infirmary, where she goes to visit her mother and I visit with Aunt Nette and Aunt Jetje[2], who happen to have beds across from each other on the ward. Of course I drop in on them as often as I can. They are getting good care.

Aunt Jetje is a dear, always cheerful and contented. She has adjusted well to the circumstances and is the darling of the ward. She is fortunate in that she brought quite a bit of luggage, so she is able to manage quite well. Aunt Nette has received your various packages, and wishes me to thank you most kindly. However, since she spends most of her time in bed and uses only a robe when she gets up, she requests no further shipments of clothing, as she has trouble storing them. She also has no need of food supplies, because she likes the meals here and they are adequate for her. What she would enjoy, perhaps, is some candy every now and then, something like crackers or hard candy that she could suck on. The same holds for Aunt Jetje. I took her some of my own cookies and chocolates this week. Come to think of it, if you send some for Aunt Jetje, it might be better to address the package to me. I shall make sure she gets it.

Lé sent me a scrumptious bag of apples. Please thank him very kindly for me. I had taken one of Leny's apples to Aunt Nette a couple of times and she enjoyed them greatly. This week I slaved over a pot of porridge for her. In the process, my green coat almost fell victim to the fire. It just barely escaped being incinerated and was badly scorched. Aunt Nette, however, did not even touch her porridge as she had enjoyed her lunch so much, so she shared it with Aunt Jetje. I may be able to sneak them a bit of hot cocoa tonight which one of the women in my barrack will try to brew for me when she has a minute. She will contribute the milk, I the cocoa cubes, and we'll share the resulting brew. She has time to do this sort of thing, since she is in the barrack all day long with her ten-month-old baby, a beautiful boy with whom I am having a love affair, of course.

Small pleasures such as these still make life quite bearable, and by doing each other little favors we can still feel much joy in being alive.

Tonight we are going en masse to big Finy to celebrate her birthday. I am glad that Lize[3] can come along. Little Roza is doing fine, too. Lize suffered a bad asthma attack this week and we hope it won't recur. Would it be possible to scrounge up a pair of boots for Lize? Perhaps some little old lady has a pair stashed away somewhere in the back of her closet. They have to be size 9½ or 10. What happened is that she has become very attached to my riding boots which I loaned her for a couple of days. Now my problem is to get them back in a civilized manner; you know I am not very good in handling sticky situations like these.

Otto is still in good health, apart from a perennial cold, a problem which he and I share. We are lucky to have good quality toilet paper, otherwise I wouldn't know what to do.

To my great relief, I am feeling well again, apart from the runny nose, that is. The sun is beginning to get spring fever! You can imagine how wonderful it is for us to have more warmth and light; on the other hand, thoughts of spring evoke memories of our beloved garden, with the big beech tree on the little hill. However, I take these memories by the scruff of the neck right away, and push them into a corner to do their sulking.

I was glad to read that our friends are well, especially Fen and Gra, but I wish they would find it in their hearts to write me a note every now and then. Your parcels arrived promptly, and I am enjoying the contents tremendously. The last one was small, but splendid. The contents were very useful: the flashlight, ink, etc. Many thanks for your kind thoughtfulness. Mother sent us some uncommonly good cookies, Selma a delicious chocolate bar—please thank them profusely for me. We also pocketed the package for Jenny, since I could not get hold of her anymore!

You must have enjoyed talking to Lé's son Klaas. They are always so kind and show such genuine interest—I talk to their relatives from time to time. I also saw Mrs. H., Paul Klein's lady friend, this week. I was happy to hear that she had had a very good trip, but she was glad to be back here, reunited with her family.

I see Neub. often—again, she expressed her gratitude for the calcium tablets. They are always a cheerful lot over there, and Walter Meijers regaled us once more with an entertaining stand-up routine of comic morning washroom stories—you know his talent as a story teller.

On rereading your letter, I come across some matters I have not touched on, so I shall answer those now, before I run out of space. For instance: blue dress received. Would you be so kind as to also send my blue cardigan with the little stars? I'm afraid it will have to be washed first and it also needs new buttons. Parmesan cheese I definitely do not want. I would like another package of figs at some time, Aukje may be able to get them if your supply has run out. The instant coffee is enticing, but if you can give it to someone who would greatly enjoy it— and it's really important—then give it to them instead. There is a sizable risk of breakage during transport anyway. Or, you could give that person a can of coffee or part of the contents of a can.

How is Daan doing these days? Otto and I talk about him often. Bella is not here: she is in Vught with Arnold, and I suppose their situation is about the same as ours. I talked to your old upstairs neighbor again. He told me he had not been able to say goodbye to you, since his departure was rather unexpected. We work together every day, as before, and he has even suggested we be on a first-name basis, which I find quite flattering.

As regards the matter of Dorus and David K's watch

chain, I know all about that, but that is neither here nor there; in fact, it makes things easier. Anyway, there is no question of great expectations, only a matter of keeping company, the right kind of company, that is, and a pleasant dinner every now and then.

[Handwritten note]

Unfortunately, I am running out of space. Have just received a summons for Nette to go on transport [illegible]. Also, all of you, please be sure to write to Jetje *soon*. Barrack #84.

Notes

1. Nanette de Jong was Gerrit's aunt, the sister of his mother.
2. Jetje Benavente-Verdoner was Gerrit's aunt, the youngest sister of his father.
3. Lize Gersons was Hilde's cousin.

[Monday, March 15, 1943]

My Dear Gait,

It looks as if it will be a fairly quiet time, as usual on Monday afternoons, so I'll make a start on a letter to you. You must have read my last letter to the Pretoriusstraat by now, and since that time not much has happened here that is worth mentioning. As before, we are doing as well as can be expected under the circumstances, and that seems to be a lot better in many respects than in the big city. We've got food and warm shelter, so none of us here have to worry about those things; and beyond those, so many things have become utterly unimportant for the time being. We do worry, of course, but to do so here is even more useless than ever before. Hence our primary task is to keep mind and body and especially our nerves in the best possible shape, and as soon as one of us catches another worrying, that person gets a good scolding all around, since wasting one's energies on worrying is not to be tolerated here. Still, in this extremely beautiful spring weather, my thoughts tend to drift off every now and then to all those activities which these lovely, sunny March days would otherwise tempt me to take up. I am more certain than ever before that long walks through the woods will indisputably be more important than spring cleaning of rooms and closets, in case we are ever in a position to make those choices again.

A tiny bit of rain one of these nights would be very welcome, though, because on a windless day like today we can enjoy the warm sunshine without discomfort, but if there is even the smallest amount of wind it gets very dusty around here after the long dry spell.

I have finally exchanged my green suit with the full skirt for the purple dress: the latter, however, makes me look like a stuffed sausage, to my dismay, and if this trend continues, I am very concerned about my summer wardrobe, which will surely be much too tight by then. At the office, my change of attire was the topic of the day, and in the barrack my changed appearance also caused a great many comments.

Here I come with another round of requests: First, a few stars[1] to put on my blue dress and the green two-piece dress; you can probably find a couple of stars somewhere which have the tips already turned under, in my inimitable manner, so that all that remains to be done is to sew them on. Second, I had the misfortune this week to break my last comb, and I would be very grateful if you could get hold of a new one for me. I am sure it will be very difficult to buy one in a store and, moreover, these things are so terribly expensive these days and of poor quality to boot, but my mane is nothing to be proud of anyway, so you can imagine what I look like without equipment to make it a bit more presentable.

Now that we are on the subject, I paid another visit to the hairdresser this week, and he managed to create a nice curly hairdo, but you should have seen the filthy suds that came off! At the first washing, the shampoo did not foam at all, and the shampoo girl was falsely accusing it of being a new war-time formula; such an insult to my carefully hoarded shampoo! The thing was, my hair was so dirty that the soap did not have any effect at all, but with the second washing it started to foam, so my precious shampoo was rehabilitated.

From these utterly trivial trivia you can tell that there really is no earth-shaking news to report at the moment. The only thing I can relate is that in the meantime I also received your last parcel containing all the items I had requested, such as sewing thread, clean sheets and a pillow-case, and especially the scarf whose color you so artfully co-ordinated with my coat. I'd really like to know where you managed to find it, and I thank you most warmly for it.

I also enjoyed the large piece of sausage. I have already used a piece of it to invite myself for supper with Dorus to-morrow evening, for he always treats me royally when I visit him, always coaxing me into having a bite when I drop in after leaving the office. One day last week, we had a number of things, including delicious fried potatoes with meatballs, and pudding for dessert. I happen to know that he loves sausage and never gets any himself, so I am very happy that I'll be able to reciprocate for a change.

As you could tell from her thank-you card, Nette also received her parcel of delicacies last week. She has been quite well so far, and she recently had very good news from Suzy and Betty in Vittel. I'll try to drop in on her in a little while, to watch her enjoying the sunshine. Her bed happens to be on the sunny side, where she catches the sun full in her face all afternoon, so she could not have a better spot anywhere. Her appetite is always good, and if I can manage before my visit, I'll brew her a nice cup of cocoa from milk that I just "organized" this afternoon. I was in luck today: managed to get more than a liter, so Floortje and I treated ourselves to a nice cup of hot milk with instant coffee with our noon meal. That jar of instant coffee has given me great pleasure; the stuff is really delicious and I've already used quite a lot of it. As soon as I've polished it off, I'll give you a yell. In the meantime I've also consumed most of the car-bonated water. Haven't tasted the tomato juice yet, though—am saving that for a special occasion, perhaps this coming Friday or Sunday!!![2]

Ro de Groot, the current Mrs. Vrijenhoek, was thrilled when I told her that you remembered the New Year's Eve party of 1922, where she had also been a guest. I spend much time with her; she is a very sweet and sensible woman, and attractive and charming as well.

This morning I had some business at the office where Hans and Kurt work, and usually Dorus too. When I had finished my business there, Dorus just happened to have some rounds to do, i.e. see people who cannot come to the appropriate offices. That was a fine opportunity for me to trot along as an instant aide, which was a good deal better than sitting in this stuffy office on a gorgeous day. When I trooped back in after an hour's absence, Willy voiced his indignation, of course, but my neighbor had already come to the rescue at his howls and had taken dictation in the meantime.

Ellen will be in the city tomorrow, and I would like you to go and see her at the Lijnbaansgracht. She is very nice, has a quick wit, and is a joy to work with.

Tonight there will be a meeting of the *halutzim* at the school. One of our coworkers, Marinus Kan, will be the speaker, and it appears that I'll be let off from work at the regular time for a change, so I am planning to attend with Otto. There is always such an unusually cheerful mood at these meetings, as I wrote you earlier.

Our quarantine lasted only a single day, fortunately, even though another case of scarlet fever has popped up since Saturday. This quarantine business is the craziest of all crazy measures, since the contagious stage of the disease occurs always well before the outbreak.

I talked to Buby's parents yesterday; they are very well. They both look fine and are in good condition. They have excellent connections here, with Hans among others, so that it would be totally superfluous for me to offer them my assistance. At any rate, there is nothing that I could do for them. Do please tell Arthur that they are quite well, considering the circumstances, and that they both look well. Please do not think that I am writing this merely to reassure you and him—it is the truth. There is no telling, however, whether they will manage to stay around here; that may not be so easy. As I wrote before, however, they have the best possible connections, and they'll find their own way.

Lé's mother is okay too, and he'll get news about her from Attorney van den Dries. Papers are needed to show that Jacobus Beytel was Aryan, i.e. copies from the Registry of Births and so on, for himself and his parents and grandparents. For now that the father is known, it has to be established that he was Aryan, in order to prove that she is half Aryan. It would be a different matter if the father was unknown, in which case it would automatically be assumed that he was not Jewish.

With regard to the cast iron stove, I thought we had discussed that matter extensively, and I remember saying that we could not use the very large one in the Breughelstraat anyway. We had kept the medium-sized one, which used to stand in our hallway, in order to place it in the Breughelstraat if needed. Anyway, it doesn't matter very much, because you had no other use for it either, but I am almost sure that we discussed the matter.

As regards the bicycle, I am awfully surprised to hear that Ans has started using it without your knowledge. I had always assumed that you had offered it to Lé. I do not understand how Pasman could have given it away without your permission. Do tell me more about this matter, because if it was done without your knowledge, that was some *chutzpah*, in spite of all we owe him. If you would like to give it to Karl, you should say so without hesitation, for *I* was not consulted in this matter, either.

[Hand-written addition in the margins]

I am enclosing a card for Mother's birthday—would you please pick out some nice flowers to go with it, for this time perhaps one or two lovely orchids!

If you have any more news about the knapsack for Erich Marx, you'll let me know as soon as possible, won't you?

Just received last package with clean brown pull-over sweater and all the other delicacies in prime condition. Many, many thanks.

Kisses, H.

Notes

1. Starting on May 2, 1942, all Jews were required to wear a yellow star with the word "JOOD" (Jew) on it at all times, even in the camps.
2. This refers to birthday celebrations: Friday, March 19, 1943, was Fran's sixth birthday; Sunday, March 21, was Hilde's mother's birthday.

[Monday, March 22—24, 1943]

My Dear Gerrit,

Phew! It took awfully long for your last letter to arrive—I have just received it. It appears that one of your letters got lost in the mail again, as I had surmised in the meantime, since the letter which you said you wrote on Monday night never got here, and the one you started on Thursday evening and continued on Friday evening is the first one I received since the meeting with Kl. It did get here very quickly though, because today is Monday evening the 22nd, so it reached me without delay. You can imagine how I just about threw myself at it, and how very happy I was to read that all of you are well and in good health, apart from Mrs. Krieker's slight indisposition, which I hope has improved in the meantime. I have to admit that I was not seriously worried about you or the others: if there had been any bad news, I would undoubtedly have heard. But when it took so long for the next letter to arrive, I realized once more how miserable it is to be without mail for so long, even if there is no earth-shaking news to be expected in the long-anticipated letters.

This past week, on Friday I believe, I paid another quick visit to your boss, as I usually do if I have the chance on the days that he is here, and he, too, told me that you are all right. He is always very friendly, even though I can take only a few minutes of his precious time. He was so kind as to tell me that you were back to working hard and regularly, from which he deduced that you did not have quite so many worries now and were also less nervous. That was wonderful news for me, of course. Even better, however, was your message that Mrs. Sch. is most likely to meet her husband here in the near future. I hope it will really happen this time. I find myself wondering, however, if her rest-cure will not be affected adversely by this, and whether she will be able to continue the cure without interruption. Well, they will have to take that chance, I suppose.

While I'm at it, I want to confirm receipt of your various packages, which got here promptly. They were great. Those, too, were a sign that you are still in the best of health, thank goodness. I did, however, deduce from the inventory written by Herta, that you must be terribly busy again. I have not even picked up your very last parcel yet, because I only got the receipt for it this evening just before starting my evening shift. I am sure that it will be as splendid as the others—the things you send me are always very much appreciated.

I was delighted with the can of applesauce, which we consumed the very day we received it, which was yesterday, Sunday, Mother's birthday. Bella and Otto were having dinner with their friends Esther and Hans Asscher-Pinkhof, and I was invited for the occasion. I brought along the can of applesauce, and we mixed the contents with a jar of strawberries which you had sent me earlier and which I had kept on purpose, hoping to combine it with applesauce. It was a most unusual treat, and all of us enjoyed it tremendously. The rest of the dinner was not to be sneezed at either: canned chanterelle mushrooms as appetizers, then a very good potato salad made from camp potatoes and decorated with a Star of David cut from a large carrot, and various open-faced sandwiches with sardines in tomato sauce, cheese, etc. After the applesauce a nice cup of tea with real kieschelish[1] which Esther Asscher-Pinkhof had received from home. Of course we toasted all the various friends and relations back home in Amsterdam with every dish we ate. These Aschers are a very young couple, originally from

Apeldoorn, where he worked as a *halut* in horticulture. Otto already knew them back then.

I would be really sorry if the lost letter never shows up, as I gather that it contains much interesting news which I am very eager to hear, after your last meeting with our friend Kl. Anyway, I hope that you will be able to tell me everything yourself in the near future.

On Friday I had myself prettied up again, in honor of Frankie's birthday. After a wonderful hot shower I went to the hairdresser to have my mane washed and tamed. Even though it had been only two weeks since I'd had it done, my hair could stand another washing; it had been so dusty the last few days that the suds that came off were filthy. After that, I received callers, Otto and Bella and a few neighbors from the barrack, Floortje Kool among them, of course, who continues to be my faithful bunk mate. For this festive occasion, to toast Frankie's health, I broke open the box of Patria crackers. It was another unusual treat, and everyone exclaimed that they were so delicious and so wonderfully fresh, as if they had been freshly baked yesterday. So I hope you got to eat some too in the meantime, for after all they used to be your very favorite cookies!!

I was also very happy with the loaf of Swedish bread, half of which I ate right away at breakfast yesterday. If you could get another one again sometime, I would very much appreciate receiving it, and I would also like you to send me a loaf of plain black rye bread, not too large, since it tends to get moldy quickly here, and *not* sliced either, as the sliced loaf usually is already moldy upon arrival. Also I would be very pleased with a bottle of really good salad dressing, to make a potato salad every now and then from left-over camp potatoes; you know I love potato salad. It would also be a change from the ubiquitous mush. There should be a bottle of good, pre-war salad dressing in the bookcase, or otherwise in the linen closet, where there ought to be more applesauce, too. Or otherwise at Animalkens, as I wrote you before. Please let me know how they are, and whether you ever see her or Miss Puper[2].

I am very glad that you are trying to get me senna *peas* (not senna leaves), because I need them badly, probably also because of the lack of exercise, what with my sedentary job. Miss Vonk may be able to provide a bag of prunes at some time, I suppose, and if so, send me a pound of those, please. I could soak them for a day or so and don't have to cook them; that would be easy enough to do. Mother's little white saucepan still comes in very handy; everyone raves about its being so practical, and people want to borrow it all the time to make a hot drink or cook some pudding.

Last week I managed to take some hot cocoa to Nette again, which she enjoyed, although she does not lack for food. She would like something tasty for her sandwiches though. Yesterday I took her a can of fish paté and half of that piece of processed cheese which you had sent me in the last parcel; it was delicious, by the way. But you do not have to send so much cheese for me, since I am not that fond of it, except perhaps on black bread. I prefer almost anything to cheese, as you may not (!) remember; moreover, we fairly often get a quite reasonable cheese here at camp. What I do keep longing for is fresh fruit, especially apples. Do ask Lé to send me some again, for the shipment from Leny and Hans is finished.

Another thing that is always a hit are the large Forto cakes. I am always very happy to have these, especially because they occasionally make good gifts for people. Last night I took two of them to the hospital when I went to visit a neighbor from the Marnixstraat who had borne a baby son here last week. Unfortunately, the woman was quite sick, poor thing. She had a beautiful baby but she herself was running a high fever and had all sorts of problems with infected nipples and obstructed milk ducts. Perhaps Aukje could select a few baby suits and a little coat and hat—all size one—from the square cardboard box and send them to me; there was a blue crocheted outfit which would be very suitable, plus some other things. But tell her to be sure and seal the box again, because of the moths.

Speaking of babies, how is Gra? I haven't had a single letter from her anymore unfortunately. I would have expected a letter from her a long time ago, even though she did not receive a direct reply from me to her letter of about two months ago.

Last Friday, we ceremoniously celebrated our three months' "anniversary" here. Of our group of about eighty people, only a very few are left, no more than about ten.

Yesterday there was another big upheaval here, and I was horrified to find Hendrien and Metha at an altogether wrong address![3] Dorus and I immediately went to see them this morning; we can get away with that every now and then in the course of the week. I took them a jar of jam right away which they were very happy to have, and this afternoon I'll bring them a loaf of bread. It is almost certain that they will leave this coming Tuesday, unless both of them were to land in the hospital, which is unlikely. Fortunately they have enough clothes and blankets, but you must send a few extra packages of butter and some jam right away to my address, also some sausage and cheese if possible, for them to take along on the journey. I was happy to hear that they had talked to all of you quite a bit recently, and that so far everything is going well for all of you; naturally, I was very surprised to get this news from them in person, which is something I had not expected at all. Don't worry too much about their impending journey—it is not supposed to be so bad after all, and anyway, there is nothing one can do but resign oneself to it.

In the meantime, another whole clan of Vellemans has collected here: Sander and his wife and Lehman[4] with daughter Sara and her fourteen-year-old son. So, if you really do come here for business, you may not have enough time to pay all the necessary personal visits.

Yesterday morning I happened to talk to Zoetedorp for a few minutes; what a very nice guy he is. He told me that his in-laws had unexpectedly arrived with the transport on Monday evening, and he was very upset about it. It is too bad that nothing can be done about such cases anymore. Ah well, one would like to keep everyone here until the end of the war, but who knows whether those who have gone on will not find themselves in a position of having to come to our aid later. The strangest thoughts and reflections often come to my mind here.

As you must have realized, I have been working on this letter for three days now, and I really hope to finish it this time without further interruptions.

I just talked to Mrs. Klaas whom I had been trying to find for several days—it was an enjoyable reunion of course. So now I shall take my time and add a few more lines. I have just discovered that I can pass along the message regarding Hendrien and Metha by way of Herman, so as far as that is concerned there is no more reason to rush this letter.

Whenever I walk to or from my job in the balmy sunshine, I dwell on all the pleasant things I'd like to talk with you about, and I make up my mind to write you a really pleasant letter for a change. But then, when I sit down to write amidst the deafening clatter of typewriters all around me, all pleasant thoughts fly out the window, and it takes the greatest effort to put together even a reasonably coherent letter.

I cannot get over this incredibly beautiful spring. It is wonderful that the weather continues to be so beautiful and sunny; only I can't resist the temptation to escape from the dusty, smelly office from time to time. Herman will tell you, no doubt, that I was a very unfaithful secretary to him, but that is also due to the fact that I have to go to the clinic three times a week for heat treatments for my arm, which has started to bother me again. I haven't noticed any improvement yet, and am still trying to get ultra violet treatments which are certain to be more effective. However, there is always a long waiting list of children with rickets for that treatment, and of course I would not want to take the place of one of them.

I was so happy to hear about the swimming lessons. How I would have loved to enjoy the sight myself! But let me be content that she[5] at least still gets the opportunity. I am also pleased that her school work is going so well and am hoping for another little note.

I would like to ask you to send my blue spring coat one of these days, as I believe I can finally bear to let go of my green winter coat. It will cause somewhat of a stir around here, but that is a chance I'll have to take! Please have it "decorated"[6] first!!

Did you receive my last shipment of dirty laundry? I apologize for the messy packing, but it had to be done in a terrible hurry and the towels hadn't even been dried yet after my shower. I was sorry to see that my good wool stockings had faded so much in the laundry, and I keep my fingers crossed that the second pair will return from laundering unscathed. They must have been sitting in the suds too long, or maybe it was too hot; at any rate the color had turned all strange and blotchy, to my grief. Enough of this, I may be able to buy new ones by the time I have to wear them again, because the season for wool stockings is happily over now. For the time being, I shall keep them at the bottom of my linen closet, clothes closet, shoe closet, etc.

This week I had the great misfortune to break two combs in a row, and I would be much obliged if you could dig up another one of those instruments for me. Preferably a good comb with a handle of course, otherwise a regular comb, but a very coarse one, please! I also would like a little bit of brilliantine. I seem to remember that there was a bottle with some left in it near the bathroom sink, or otherwise in the medicine chest.

Talking about bottles, I do have to rave about the "tomato juice" which I opened in the meantime. Though not as much fun as drinking it while sitting around our faithful black stove, it was quite good anyway, and very agreeable, with an especially beneficial effect on the telephone connection!!!!![7]

This week I spent a pleasant evening with Herz. There were several other people, Joseph Weisz and his sweet and very charming wife; Mrs. Helbing from the Bussumergrindweg, where Annalieze Frijda was; and her tenant Gerhard Frank, who is very highly regarded here (the latter, of course) and who accordingly has a prominent position. It was an unusual sensation once again to sit around a table under a lamp with a small group of people, to be drinking tea (sorry, it was coffee) from a regular cup, and without seeing a crowd of people shuffling by all the time; and to be able to keep up a conversation without being interrupted, without having to get up all the time to let someone pass to climb into his bed which just happens to be behind the bench you're sitting on.

Arthur's parents are doing very well, too, except that it is still quite uncertain whether their efforts to stick around here will be successful. Let's hope that they will be—so far it looks fairly good.

Lé's mother is all right, too. I happened to see her this morning while she was taking a stroll in the sunshine. She is lucky to have friends among the older residents, so that she always has company and somewhere to walk to.

How are Barend's parents doing? I heard that they had been totally confused for a couple of weeks, but people who were in the sanatorium with them maintain that they were still there, for the time being. Did you know anything about that?

Rudi and Berthold's Uncle Jo and Aunt Sally left yesterday, there was nothing anyone could do about it, even though they were fast friends of Zimmern, who is quite a VIP here after all. Please give kindest regards to my father from Mrs. Massé, who was hospitalized with a very sophisticated gall-bladder attack just in the nick of time[8]. Perhaps Father could write her a little note some time, at Pavilion

#5 of the hospital. My impression is that she gets sufficient supplies of food.

Had I written you that Nette is now in Barrack #81? She received all the parcels promptly and in good order, so the mail apparently is being forwarded automatically.

All our friends and acquaintances of course always send their best regards to all of you.

Yesterday Roosje returned, and to my delight brought good and pleasant news about all of you. How nice that she just happened to drop in on Mother's birthday, and that there was such a festive room full of visitors and flowers, just as there used to be. She was quite enamored of the whole *mishpoche*[9]. It was apparently at Father's request (who had obviously made a deep impression on her), that she paid her second visit, and was able to give Mother some more detailed information. She is one of the nicest girls in the secretarial pool here; all the others are so self-important and put on such airs, and you know I cannot stand that.

I am slowly nearing the end of my meaningless scribbling, but this is just about the best I can do under the circumstances. I can't write you extensively about everything anyway, and those things that I can write you about are rather superficial and uninteresting, at least so it seems to me. Are you vitally interested in the fact that I am ready to receive a new shipment of figs? Aukje could arrange for them if you should have run out. I may even have written this in a previous letter; if so, then skip this paragraph. Oh dear, I am obviously getting quite corny, and in addition you have to swallow a heavy dose of typos. Oh well, they won't really upset your digestion.

How is Bé? I would really like to try and write her again, but at the moment I do not have the peace of mind to write her a cheerful letter, and anyway, you keep her posted on all the goings-on, I am sure.

I was much relieved that Daan was not on yesterday's transport, for it was quite a group coming in, more than one hundred. No one I knew, however, except for Metha and Hendrien, but that was more than enough for me!

I talk to Dorus almost daily; in fact, he has some business in our office these days in connection with his duties.

Another exceedingly interesting tidbit is that I was awfully pleased with the lovely bar of Maya soap you included in the parcel. As it happened, I had just started using a new piece that very morning, so it really made me smile to find this new bar in the package. Now I have one in reserve again. They last me about three or four weeks, which is rather long, but I only wash my hands two or at most three times a day, usually only in the mornings and in the evenings, as I don't have time during the day and anyway, your hands are filthy again in no time. Moreover, it is too much trouble to climb up on my bunk to retrieve my soap and towel each time, and then it is another two hundred feet to the faucet!!! You don't have to send me soap powder anymore, as I rarely launder anything here, and if I do, I use the camp soap which is perfectly adequate for the purpose. You already know that it is "no" to tomato ketchup, but "yes" to salad dressing.

Should I start trying to get a suitcase sent in this direction? And if so, which one? Probably my good leather accordion suitcase would be the best. It is tough and otherwise I might not get to use it for quite a while. If I should have to leave it behind soon, in case of departure direction Trompenberg[10], I might have to do without it for the rest of my days.

I am re-reading your letter and just ran into the herring salad. On paper, that is, since in real life I'm sorry to say I've not had the pleasure; I wouldn't mind having some for a change. Our barrack may be too high-class to qualify for something like that. It is true that no one in my barrack is short of bread or butter, the basic stuff, a very unusual phenomenon for this place, as you can imagine.

I read that Selma works there too, and I hope she does not take that too seriously and does not get too tired, because one should have no illusions about the useful effect of one's efforts. The Jewish Council *Ausweisz* is not worth a nickel here, not even the Jewish Council *Sperre*[11] on the I.D., and in any case she will certainly not be able to get that one anymore. It gives you a tiny bit of protection as long as you are still in Amsterdam, but here it does not count at all. I just hope that it will continue to give protection in Amsterdam for a long time. How is Paul? Too bad that his stomach is giving him so much trouble. I hope he is keeping a strict diet and staying as calm as possible.

About the package for Kurt: I haven't heard any more than you, but then, he has been quite "invisible" for the past few weeks and as it happens I haven't talked to him for at least four or five weeks either.

Jo Vrijenhoek's husband is not here since he is Aryan. We had to laugh about your description of Izzy and Jo Polak!

I am very curious about the visit to Fen. Have they received my note and could they decipher it?

How wonderful that you wrote such a beautiful poem for Yoka again—she always appreciates it so much. I am sometimes envious because I cannot write as well as you; isn't that childish of me? But I am glad for their sake that you do have the ability and have such a hidden talent for poetry.

In the meantime, I am already longing for your next letter, because I assume that you will have a lot of news to report after the last meeting with Klaas. I am very happy that there is a chance that you may start in your new position soon, and I hope that it will materialize in the very near future.

I enjoyed reading the story of Lotte's[12] *chupah* once again, but I remembered it very well from a letter which Aunt Selma had let me read once, or in which Aunt Selma had told us about it. How is Paul? I hope that he has improved some in the meantime and that he will be altogether well soon. They should not worry so much, because first of all, things always turn out differently from the way you think, and second, nerves certainly play a big part in his illness, even though he was always quite cheerful and optimistic in recent years.

What is the situation regarding the spring wardrobe of the trio? It is really hard for me that I am not in a position to do anything about that at this time and in addition some of the clothes must be outgrown by now. Has that blue suit from Aukje been taken out of storage? It is sure to fit now. How I wish I could see how he looks in it! Sometimes, at night, when we're already in bed, I hear the familiar sound of tinkling into a potty and then my thoughts fly back to the little blue pajamas which we got from Burmann in Groningen at the time. Those must be getting a bit tight too, now, so Frankie's hand-me-downs will have to do, if still usable. There is probably a new toothbrush for Otje at the bottom of Aukje's suitcase, and there should be one of those special brushes with a black handle which I always liked, and of which I would like one to keep in reserve, if possible. There are two beautiful new pairs of interlock pajamas for Yoka in the suitcase marked V.S. [Hilde's initials are Verdoner-Sluizer] (flat suitcase) and for the time being Frankie can use those that Yoka has outgrown. The weather is getting right for the nice new knee socks, and I hope that all of them have enough of those.

Also in Aukje's suitcase is the rust-brown pullover sweater that I had started to knit eons ago. Perhaps you can have it sent here sometime, together with all the wool, or otherwise send the wool in installments to avoid the chance of all of it getting lost. The reason is that Ro Vrijenhoek has plenty of time and has offered to knit it for me. It was patterned after the beautiful sweater from Maison de Bonneterie, which, by the way, I would like to have here eventually, with a skirt to go with it, possibly the gray one after it has been laundered.

What would you suggest I do with my heavy winter clothes which I won't need for quite a while? Shall I ask for a suitcase to be brought here to store them in, possibly with mothballs? It is perhaps best to keep them here, to have them within reach at all times.

As regards the riding boots, I do not miss them so much anymore, as long as Lize gets good wear out of them, and the money is not important. I am so happy that Rudi and Berthold[13] are probably going to fare better [than I feared]; that far outweighs the loss of a pair of shoes. You must look at it this way: when I heard that Rudi and Berthold were safe, I was happy to sacrifice that pair of riding boots as a sort of token passage paid for their safety. As I said before, I do not miss the boots at all anymore, and if I should ever have to move on from here, I certainly could not take ski boots, riding boots and overshoes, not even to mention the various pairs of sturdy oxfords that I have here.

Have you talked to Roosje (from the Blasiusstraat) in the meantime? She had promised to send a message to the Pretorius to request that someone from there would come and see her, as she cannot possibly go around to all the addresses of her colleagues' friends. I had given her the additional message that I would like to have one of those practical jam buckets with handle (and lid, of course), a plain tin bucket which would be ideal to transport the "organized" milk and other stuff in, and also would serve handily to heat it, since these buckets heat very quickly on the stove.

I have received the tonic, thank you, but I haven't used it yet. Those spells of extreme fatigue may have had something to do with spring, for ever since I've had the tonic, I'm much less tired, just from looking at it! With the continued bright and balmy weather one does not tire so easily.

I would like you to send me some senna peas. There may be a bag of them somewhere in the baby dresser; if not, you can get some at the drugstore or pharmacy. Will you also ask for Kola-Astier? I am sure that would be good for you, too, especially since you seem to be suffering from drowsiness and fatigue sometimes, as I have gathered from your letters. You should try it, really!

There is absolutely no rush for the leg bandages, also because my fatigue is much better these days.

I definitely have not received the first letter, in which you wrote about Ro de Groot, but sometimes letters lie around the post office for a while, so it is possible that I may still get it one of these days.

I haven't talked to Weisz in the past few days, so I haven't heard a thing yet about the parcel you sent to his son. Would you please send another package to the Bachrachs, for their little son, Barrack #47E. He happens to be my milk connection and therefore terribly important to me; moreover, both of them, he and his wife, are always very friendly and generous.

I am sorry that there is no chance of matzos, but I suppose we will survive without them too. I, for one, won't shed a tear about it. On the other hand, I would like another loaf of black rye, if it is not too hard to get. The round bread with poppy seed looks delicious, but I haven't cut it yet. I think I'll also take that tomorrow night when I go for supper. Those little challa loaves were wonderful too, and just today I ate the last piece of the lot you sent me about two weeks ago. They do not get stale very quickly and keep their good flavor to the last crumb.

I haven't spoken to Kurt yet after receipt of your parcel, but I'll let you know as soon as I hear anything. What about the plans of Veertje's father[14] to come and visit here sometime? I am not sure of this, but I have heard rumors that it has become quite difficult lately to get permission to visit.

I certainly received the package with the two types of sausage in good condition and I like the new type of sausage almost better even than the old one. How are meat supplies in the city? I really hope it is okay.

I'd also like to know about the matter of Henk's rug. If he would like to sell it and you also think that is a good idea, you should make the decision. If it is not necessary, I would not rush into the sale, though.

I also wanted to tell you how much use I get out of your flashlight, even though the days are longer now and we are getting better street lights all the time. Every evening the row of street lights that runs along the the main streets has been extended with one or more blue lights. So you must keep the Bijou flashlight for yourself, for I definitely do not need it. Neither do you, it occurs to me as I am writing this!

And, lastly, I would like to ask you to include a dust cloth in one of the parcels some time, so I can give the stack of boxes and packages a good cleaning. Up till now it has only been dusted "by force of mouth"!! I am a truly tidy housewife, don't you think? You just can't keep a good housewife down!!!

At long last, dear Gait, my long-winded tale is drawing to a close, and my final request is to give my very best to all good friends and relations. To Father and Mother in the first place, also to the Kriekers and thank them warmly for their very kind letter. I'll have the morning off tomorrow and I am definitely planning to visit his brother in #63. Is he still here?

How are Wim and Else? Please also give them my regards and especially Jan and Fen where I'll be in my thoughts often during this week!! Has Frans received my letter and was she able to read it? What a milestone, and so far away!!!

It is not necessary for you to send anything to Asch or Neuburger, as they are adequately supplied from all sides.

[Hand-written addition in the margins]

On re-reading I notice that I have been rambling again, especially here at the end, but that is because every time I re-read part of your letter, something occurs to me that needs mentioning.

Well, dear Gait, this is enough for today, I suppose. I

just dropped in on Nette, who had received Bea's card with Mother's last letter. Guess who is the doorman of her barrack? May from the Hague, who later moved to Oisterwijk. We had seen his wife Gretel and their son as late as June or July or thereabouts at Jops and Ba's.

They are good friends of Mo's, and I believe that they were the manufacturers of [illegible]. I had met his father, May Sr., here earlier, but he has left in the meantime. His wife works very hard as a nurse. They are terribly nice, as they always were, and send you their very best regards.

There are always so many people who give me best regards for my husband or for my parents: Erich Ziegler among them, that wonderful pianist of the Nelson Revue, and Hermann Ehrlich of the Tuschinski Theatre and lots of others. Bye-bye now! Lots of love and a thousand kisses.

Do you ever hear anything from Miss Puper or Animalkens, Aimee, etc?

How is the censoring [. . .] for [. . .] in Hilversum? Are you having a great deal of trouble getting hold of everything? According to what I hear here, everything is getting much more difficult. Haven't you heard anything from Rudi and Berthold yet? They really left a great void here! I miss them more every day!

I wanted to ask you, if you send me another clean sheet, please do not send one with scalloped edge but rather with the diamond monogram. Those are of a heavier fabric and they do not wrinkle so much. Preferably with matching pillowcase!

Has my gray skirt been washed yet? I would like to have that suit sent here with the beautiful blue sweater and also the coral necklace! Also a suitcase, please, as we are going to be moved to another barrack soon.

Just received last two splendid parcels in their entirety. No butter, alas! Everything else wonderfully taken care of! Many thanks!

Notes

1. *Kieschelisch* is a pastry of deep fried dough sprinkled with powdered sugar, enjoyed by Dutch Jews during the festival of Purim, in March.
2. Animalkens is a code name for Miss Dierkens, Fran's kindergarten teacher; "dier" in Dutch means animal. Miss Puper was Yoka's first-grade teacher.
3. No doubt the Punishment Barrack from which inmates were deported on the very next transport.
4. Lehman Velleman was Gerrit's uncle, married to his mother's sister, Anna de Jong.
5. This paragraph refers to Yoka.
6. By "decorated" Hilde means have a yellow star sewn on.
7. A euphemism. Hilde often asks for prunes, figs, and senna peas to alleviate constipation.
8. Mrs. Massé's gall bladder attack saved her from having to go on transport as she must have been declared "unfit for travel," unlike Jo and Sally, mentioned previously, who "left yesterday." For a while, hospitalization was one way to delay going on transport.
9. *Mishpoche* is the Hebrew word for family.
10. The home address in Hilversum was Trompenbergerweg 45. Perhaps Hilde is alluding to an escape, i.e. "going home."
11. *Ausweisz* and *Sperre* were two classifications of deferment stamps doled out by the Nazis through the Jewish Council. They were only temporarily effective, if at all; sooner or later everyone was to be deported.
12. Charlotte Wallman, Hilde's cousin, the daughter of Selma and Paul Wallman, lived in Palestine. *Chupah* refers to her wedding.
13. Berthold, Rudi, and Lize Gersons were Hilde's cousins, three of the four children of her mother's sister, Henriette. Berthold and Herman survived the war, Rudi and Lize did not. Berthold's wife, Finy, and son also died.
14. Karl Brandt. Vera, or "Veertje," is one of his daughters. Hilde avoids using Karl's name to protect him.

April 9, 1943

Dear Mother, Father, Selma and Paul,

Today is our letter-writing day and I have not even had time yet to start a letter to you. Of course I don't want to pass up this opportunity to let you know that we are doing all right, fortunately, and that we are in good health as usual and are enjoying our work. The only drawback is that work tends to take up all our time, so that we rarely get to visit with our friends.

After work, at about 6:30 p.m. and often later, I run to the hospital to pay a few visits, and if we haven't had our hot meal at 1 p.m., I miss out on that. This has been happening pretty often lately, for by the time I get back, the meal has got cold and it is such a problem to get it heated up. On the other hand, if I eat first, visiting hours at the hospital are over by the time I get there.

Aunt Kee[1] has been pretty much all right so far. I helped her pack her backpack with the clothes that had been sent to her in a suitcase. Fortunately, she was very well provided with underwear, a warm woolen dress and sturdy shoes; she also enjoyed the food. But she was very worried about Albert, as she hadn't had any news from him for as long as she had been here; from this we gather that he is no longer in Amsterdam either. Otto and I have of course visited her every evening we could, which she appreciated very much.

I was unable to visit Mrs. Massé the past few days, since her ward is still under quarantine because of scarlet fever. I am happy to report that she looks well, but was in much pain from her gall bladder. Rest will probably take care of it.

And how are things with all of you, and especially how is Uncle Paul's health? I hope that he is a bit better and that he can now take full advantage of the lovely spring sunshine again. I can really picture you enjoying your nice big balcony where you can sit undisturbed.

The Kriekers had to tell us all the latest gossip from the neighborhood of course; they also told us how many visitors you had on your birthday, dear Mother, and what lovely flowers. I also hope that you were able to celebrate Selma's birthday together, and I heard from Krieker that she even received a birthday cable from Grete[2], beautifully on time as usual. What about Paul and Selma's plans to visit her sometime? Have the four of you given that matter any thought lately, and perhaps discussed it with the good friends at the Van Eijckstraat? That might be interesting, you know.

Of course it was wonderful to talk to Gerrit again at long last, and I hope that the trip was not too hard on him. It was quite exhausting for him, especially this last time, I think, even though he left fit and in good spirits. Because of all the pressing business and all the messages he had to take care of we were extremely busy, but I do believe that all in all it was very useful for him to have had some personal contact once again with the various people.

I also talked to the mother of his colleague Dave yesterday, and I helped her as much as I could; I managed to get her a few blankets, as she had not received her own blankets yet.

Last night I also dropped in on Aunt Mietje, who was just being admitted to the hospital with a very upset stomach. She will receive much better care there of course. Uncle Sam is doing fine, I am happy to say. He stops by the office every now and then and always comes by to say hello to me. In spite of the fact that he has to do without some of his usual creature comforts he is adjusting very well here. It may be a good thing for him that he lives in the same barracks as Kriekers, as this gives him yet another person to talk to, even though he has found plenty of other old friends and relations as well.

Last week I sent you some empty boxes which I did not need anymore, because you are always clamoring for packing material. Have you received them? Now that Mrs. Krieker is no longer at the Breughelstraat, I would also like to send you my dirty laundry if possible, if I don't get around to laundering it myself here. It is never very much, for I use clean clothes very sparingly here, but you could send the bed linens to Burgers along with the other laundry, which would leave only a few silk camisoles and underpanties for you to wash. I hope this is not asking too much, as I cannot expect Gerrit's mother to do it for me and the underwear is quickly destroyed if it is sent to the laundry!

Of course we were very happy to receive your recent letters; we always very much enjoy reading your quotations, dear Father, which are always so very true and to the point. The quote from Multatuli, for instance, really hit the nail on the head; one should always look at one's work in that light, here more than ever, and then things will still turn out all right.

Have you talked to Gerrit since Monday? I am already longing for another letter from you, for by now you are about the only ones who send me a note every now and then, now that Gerrit tells me everything in person.

Today I received another wonderful package from Lé, which I was extremely happy to have as it contained all sorts of fresh food such as apples, carrots and , best of all, three lovely heads of lettuce, which I had for lunch right away with some salad dressing that Gerrit had just sent me in his last package. You will probably not be surprised to hear that I devoured all that lettuce at one sitting, for such things are a rarity here, and from time to time one gets a real craving for such fresh greens. What was it again that Aunt Selma used to make as a sandwich spread from creamed butter and a hard-boiled egg and some onion? Could you whip up some of that again some time and send us a jar of it?

Today I managed to make another pudding which we plan to have for dessert tonight after the pea soup. Floortje and I are already looking forward to it. Would you please ask Gerrit to send me a few packages of pudding mix and possibly some cocoa, so I can make a chocolate pudding one of these days, with the cornstarch which I still have. Do you ever manage to get any onions? If so, you may send me one every now and then, to make fried potatoes.

This letter is even duller than usual I am afraid; but I have really experienced so very little that is worth writing about that it is about time to end it; otherwise this letter might not make the outgoing mail, and the next letter day is not until two weeks from today, as you know.

This afternoon I saw Otto for a few minutes; he is off work for a few days because he hurt his finger. It is nothing to worry about fortunately, but it does give him time to keep me company at lunch for a change. He told me that he had just received your last package and one from the Jewish Council at the same time, which was most welcome as they had been quite short of bread for a couple of days. So this serves as an acknowledgment that those two packages have been received in good order. Would you please also tell Lé that I am very grateful for his last shipment. Because of all the visits I had to pay, I haven't had a chance to visit his mother for a while, and I'll see if I can manage to do so tonight at long last, after the various hospital patients. I did see her walking around the other day, so I know that she is all right.

I took half a loaf of bread and a piece of ginger cake to Aunt Nettchen this week, which she could really use. However, it's no longer necessary for you to send her anything anymore.

1943   **149**

This past week we had a terrible storm. It was so bad that a piece of roof flew through the air like a flying carpet out of *A Thousand and One Nights* and landed on the road with a bang. Luckily, there were no casualties, just the scare. But lying in bed you could hear the storm raging and imagine yourself at sea in mid-ocean.

Well, my dear ones, my writing is not very inspired today, so you will have to take this for what it is.

Please pass this letter on to Gerrit right away; and I hope to get another long letter from you very soon.

[Hand-written addition]

My very best to all of you and I want you to know I think of you very often.

A thousand kisses to all,
Hilde

Notes

1. Kee Suikerman-Sluizer was Hilde's aunt, the sister of her father; she had two sons, Jules and Albert.
2. Margharete Wallman was Hilde's cousin, the daughter of Paul and Selma Wallman. During the war she lived in Buenos Aires with her husband and became a citizen of Argentina.

Loose hand-written sheet of undetermined date.

In the mean time it is Thursday, and while the repair-man is cleaning my machine I have some time left to add a few lines by hand, for several more things have occurred to me, too many to scribble in the narrow margins.

I just talked to Mr. Katz, who has been back here since last night and who gave me your regards. He, too, had been through the emotional wringer again, and in view of his stories I must insist *most emphatically* that Paul and Selma *definitely and absolutely* should sleep upstairs from now on, especially now that the cold weather has passed. That will be ever so much safer for them and any objections that might stand in the way of their doing so should be cleared away immediately, even if it should entail throwing all the junk that is stored there now out of the attic window and onto the street right away. Nothing could be more urgent than arranging this *immediately*. For Katz it was also the fact that they slept upstairs that saved him, even though in his case he probably would have been released again, if only after an eight-day stay at Fen's neighbors[1], which is what happened to some of his roommates. However, Paul and Selma would *definitely* not be so lucky! Please write to me by return mail what the plans are with regard to this; I really hope that my advice will not go unheeded.

Now your patience has probably been exhausted, and I

just hope that my report is not so dull that it cannot hold your attention!

Is there ever a chance of getting hold of another jar of peanut butter? I was never very fond of it before, but here I have suddenly begun to enjoy it very much, as did Otto and Bella, to whom I gave the jar after I had eaten more than half of the contents. Our barrack leader, who was not familiar with the stuff, also would drop by at breakfast time every now and then to enjoy a bite of it. He is always so kind and solicitous of our welfare that we are always pleased to be able to reciprocate with a small favor. I do so hope that you will find a decent comb for me soon, for it is quite a struggle every day to tidy up my hair with a fragment.

Now that the weather is getting warmer, I would also like to have the second silk nightgown from Aukje. I wrote about this before, I mean the short-sleeved one with a bobbed collar.

Please send the senna peas soon and some dried prunes as well, and if you ever can spare some of that old-fashioned tomato juice, I'd really like some of that, too, for I use it for "medicinal purposes," to enhance the effect of the figs!

[In the margins]

Aren't you lucky to have a bicycle permit still! What about Yoka's bike, and the one belonging to Ans?

How do you spend your evenings these days? You probably don't see our friends very often now that you are so busy during the day and cannot go out at night.[2] It's really too bad!

Just heard from Dorus that Barend's parents have arrived here. Haven't talked to them yet! Planning to visit Metha and Hendrien again tomorrow!

Well, dear Gait, I'll write again as soon as possible, when I get a chance. Please share this letter with the Pretoriusstraat. I may use my letter day tomorrow to write Karl and Gra a postcard each. I got another very nice note from Karl yesterday. Please remind Gra to write to me soon!

1943

Notes

1. This is a reference to the "Hollandse Schouwburg".
2. People could no longer go out at night due to the 8 p.m. curfew imposed on the Jews by the Nazis after June 30, 1942.

[Monday, April 12, 1943]

Dear Gerrit,

After an unbelievably busy Sunday, it is a little quieter
now, as it frequently is on Monday afternoon, so that I have
a nice little stretch of time to bend your ear. Of course I
have not had any news from you all week, as we had arranged, but now that it appears that you will not be able to
come for a while, at least definitely not tonight, it is getting
to be a long time without news. The only sign of life from
you was the splendid package which I received yesterday in
good condition and which pleased me very much, as usual,
and for which I thank you very much. From the various
contents of the package I could deduce all sorts of things,
e.g. that Karl could still get prunes and also a can of powdered milk, which I certainly will not open until you are
here again, the more so because I have lately been successful in "organizing" milk again, since a favorable wind was
blowing around the milk containers this week. The day before yesterday I surprised Mrs. Krieker with some, so that
she could cook some porridge for her husband, and today I
am taking my catch as my contribution to dinner with
Dorus where I was invited again at long last, which hadn't
happened in at least two or three weeks.

I returned the scarf to Ro, who was very happy to have
her precious possession back and sends her kindest regards.
A new case of scarlet fever had just been diagnosed in her
room, so I am wondering whether they will also be quaran-
tined. It is going around here at an alarming rate: new cases

turn up every day, but fortunately we never hear any more about it, so I assume that the disease runs its normal course. Usually, however, the infection has already spread before the disease breaks out, so we live in fear and trepidation what the next few days will bring.

Aside from all this, tension is running very high again, as always when it is getting close to Tuesday, and this past week was also terribly stormy and turbulent, as you can probably imagine.

It is not certain yet how things will turn out for Kriekers, but I believe and hope that they will be all right for tomorrow at least. This is another reason why I am sorry that you could not come this time, as you could certainly see this matter through better, after having broached it with Hans. He was off on a trip for a few days, by the way, and I really could not bother him about it yesterday or today. The problem is that he [Krieker] is not a good enough shoemaker, and the alternative with S. which I immediately pursued is not as simple as two plus two equals four either, but involves several people. In the meantime, Ernst Menko has come to fill Hans' place [illegible word inserted by hand] which I am also very happy about, but the situation is different for him and therefore he could start right away.

You must have read my letter to the Pretoriusstraat in the meantime and gleaned a store of information from it. I was terribly upset about Aunt Kee, but it was a hopeless case which could not be helped. It would have been a blessing for her if she had died peacefully in her sleep here, for no good can possibly come of such a trip for her, but unfortunately that was not to be, and the only comfort is that her departure may have made it possible for someone else to stay here, so that she may have done someone a good turn by leaving. But of course there is no telling yet if that is so. I only hope that my father will not be too terribly upset about it, for I really think this is very hard for him to take.

I visited Nette a few days ago. She is doing well and is well provided with food and drink and in all respects gets

Signs of Life

the best possible care under the circumstances. She is fortunate to be basically healthy, apart from her leg, and that is quite something. Her leg is massaged regularly and is improving in mobility, but of course she does not have much opportunity to practice walking.

Aunt Mietje from Gouda is also in the hospital and gets regular visits from Uncle Sam, which gives him a bit of exercise and some diversion. It was quite funny, actually, that she requested oranges, Vichy water and other delicacies, in which we had to disappoint her of course.

I see the Broekmans every now and then, but I restrict the conversation to a hello, if at all possible, for I know their song by now and I do not feel like listening to the same tale of woe every time.

[Monday April 19, 1943]

I had got as far as this with my letter last week and you may not believe me when I tell you that for a whole week I could not get around to continuing the letter. All week long I waited with rising expectation for news from you, but to no avail, so that I came to the conclusion that another letter must have got lost in the mail.

But tonight I finally received your letter of Saturday with all the bad news. First, about your illness, which I had heard from Bernard Z. just a little earlier, and then about Paul and Selma, which made me feel as if I had been hit over the head with a heavy club. We know it is inevitable as long as this devilish process is going on, but when it finally happens, you feel defeated anyway. Of course I shall make sure to be there for their arrival. As it happens, I had already applied for an evening permit, as I was half expecting your visit here tonight, and I'll try to get Paul admitted to the hospital right away, even though that gives no protection whatsoever, but at least is a little more peaceful than in the barracks. Other than that, I don't know what to do and I just hope that Selma will not be feeling too desperate.

In the past few weeks, since your last visit, things have not improved: sixty extra beds were placed in every barrack, so that it actually would be a good idea to institute one-way traffic indoors, as it is practically impossible to get from one side of the barrack to the other now. During the first few days it was truly frightful, for in addition to this we were all terribly unhappy when we had to leave our nice clean 73 to be dispersed over several barracks. All the little groups that had formed in the course of time were torn apart and everybody ran around anxious and crying, and we all felt just as upset as on our first day here.

In the meantime we have gotten fairly used to the new situation and settled in with new nails and cubby holes in the rafters to hang and store our belongings. Floortje and I sleep in adjacent bunks again, now in 68, as you may have gathered from the change of address which I sent you. We have gone back to sleeping well, as usual, and we now eat up on our third floor [top-bunk] almost all the time. There we have some peace and quiet at least, and during the day we are so busy anyway that we are hardly ever in the barrack.

It wasn't very wise of you, dear Gerrit, to keep going as you did with your cold, and I am happy to hear that you got away with it fairly well, considering. I hope you have recovered in the meantime and I also hope that you will be wiser next time and not let yourself get so sick, even though I can well imagine that it is hard for you to stay in bed when you have so much to do and are wanted everywhere. It bothers me a great deal that I cannot do anything for you now and, on the contrary, that you still have to worry about me and have even arranged a beautiful package for me again. Your poor mother must be terribly busy now that she has to do everything herself, but perhaps you have found a solution to that in the meantime, for there is no way she can do all that work on her own. You must be sure to take good care and not go out too soon, especially not on the bicycle where you will work yourself into a sweat, for you really have to get well soon.

It is a comfort to know that your mother is giving you excellent care; I certainly could not do any better than she, and perhaps not even as well. But she has so many other chores to do too! Anyway, I must not think about it, otherwise I start to feel very sad and depressed and I need my strength for tonight, every little bit of it that is left. I shall be very happy if you get well enough soon to come here again, and then we'll take it a little easier, so that we'll have more time for each other. By the way, was your boss pleased with your reports of your trips and have any changes been made yet as a result?

I talked to Dé's mother a couple of times this week, but I have grave doubts about her chances tomorrow. On Tuesday of last week I sent a telegram to Dé about this matter, but haven't heard a thing from him since. He could at least have replied. The letters which Floor and he write her are not very warm either, but this is strictly between you and me of course! Please understand that I cannot possibly do anything more in this case, although I want to give it one last try. I'll have to take one more good look at the situation!

Although I have a fairly quiet period in which to write to you just now, I hardly know where to start. So many thoughts that I want to share with you go through my head, but I feel so restless and also I do not know where to start; anyway, the rapids drag us all along so fiercely that it is hard to keep afloat, and all the flotsam that comes in here is indescribable.

Things went wrong for the Kriekers, as you may have guessed or heard in the meantime. I'll tell you all about that some other time. Looking back, I did not do them a service at all, because the previous week they could have traveled together with his parents and sister. I gave them a half pound of butter to take on the trip; they were well provided otherwise. I had given them the powdered soap earlier, and at the train I ran into Kurt, who knew about them but said he could not do anything. All Denneboom's children and Van Dam from Hilversum[1] have passed through in the meantime and so on and so on. And how long will this go on? Long enough for all, I'm afraid!

I received a warm and pleasant letter from Fen, which I was very happy to have. Will you thank her profusely for it and tell her that she made me very happy. I talked to your boss for a few minutes this past week, also in connection with Dé's mother, but he could not do anything about it, or so he said.

Now I have a few more requests for you for some things that I need, namely toilet paper, of which I gave a package to the Kriekers, and I am also almost out of figs. And, I have a filthy dish towel and an equally filthy pillow case, so I would like one or two clean ones of those, please. I have not received my clean laundry from Mother yet and I hope it will arrive here before Wednesday, otherwise I shall once more be unable to send my dirty laundry this week. Why don't you send me two of those yellow towels and two white ones some time, as spares. Storage is such a problem anyhow, two or three more things won't make much of a difference. Would you please also try to get a thin night-shirt from Aukje, and I am sure that there are more pink silk camisoles in the drawer of the brown dresser, at least one that is not worn out; also a package of underpants which are not too badly mended, for I only have one here when the other one is in the laundry. Otherwise there are new ones in the trunk marked V.S., the old one that used to belong to Jopie.

I was very pleased with the food again, as usual, and enjoyed every bite. Last week I also opened that jar of delicious Palestinian honey, after liquefying it on the stove, and every time I took a taste of it, I remembered last year's disaster, when a jar exploded on the stove because Otje had pried open the bottom door of the stove with his little walking stick, which caused the stove to overheat. It has already been a year since we left the Trompenberg, what a miserable year!!! And how much longer?

Lé sent me another wonderful package of fresh fruit and vegetables: apples and carrots and a few heads of lettuce which I fixed with salad dressing and happily ate. Could you send me one or two fresh cucumbers next time, to put on my sandwiches, for variety. I do not approve at all of your sending me the jar of blueberry jam, because that happens to be so good for you, for your health, so I shall definitely keep it for you. The sausage was delicious and so much of it! I'll take another piece to Nette. I also brought her a piece of cheese this week which she enjoyed, but it certainly is not necessary, even though she does enjoy salty things. I only managed to visit her once, for we work until six-thirty and there was so much work all week that we couldn't leave on time. Then comes dinner, and visiting hours are from seven to eight-fifteen only. The move also caused quite an upheaval which kept us busy for a day and a night and had us upset for two!

Great commotion was also caused by the sudden departure of some two hundred people to Theresienstadt, which many of them are not at all happy about. The Kauffmanns whom you met here are among them. You sent them a package of butter once so far and I returned the remainder of the gw (railway cars), that is ap,wz, to them.[2] Perhaps you can still reach them, since they will have a one-day lay-over in Amsterdam, as they have been told here. You might be able to do something for them, but it is not necessary. They are very sad because they have to leave their eldest son behind here, which is a very bitter pill to swallow. There are more lucky ones like them here who are in the same painful situation.

I haven't heard whether Horst Cohen received his package, but I'll ask him in a little while, as I'm going to the parcel post office anyway. It is ten-thirty already and as I do not have anything exciting to tell you, I think I'll write the rest by hand later.

1943 161

[In handwriting]

It has gotten quite late in the meantime and I'll have another letter-writing day the day after tomorrow, and moreover there is not much news to tell. Could you send me a pair of overalls size 18? I gave mine to Kriekers to take on the trip, and just to be sure I would like to have a pair here again. I am glad that you sent two pairs of stockings along. Please initiate a search for cotton socks some time, for as soon as the weather permits I'll be wearing those again.

I very much hope that you have fully recovered in the meantime, and I am longing to see you. How are my parents? Well, I shall unfortunately hear that soon enough in person. I am trying to get Selma assigned to #68 with me. A bed below me has just been vacated, so that at least is a piece of good luck!

Lots of love and best wishes and strength. Warm regards to your parents and a thousand kisses to you.

Please pass this letter on to Grada!

Perhaps I'll write to the Pretoriusstraat again on Wednesday for a change; you'd get to read that too, after all!

Notes

1. Denneboom was a school. Bram van Dam was an educator, a close friend of Gerrit, who survived the war.
2. Meaning not clear.

[Wednesday] April 21, 1943

My Dears,

Actually I am totally exhausted from banging on the typewriter all day, from eight-thirty this morning until now, which is [ ] o'clock already, and I have felt such pressure all day because today is letter-writing day, and this letter must absolutely be handed in tonight, yet every time I [want to] start it, I have to take dictation again from one or the other of my bosses. I was very busy all week, too, so I could not get around earlier to making a head start on my bi-weekly report to you, but from Father's last letter I gathered that my previous letter was in the mail for a rather long time, so if this one travels a little faster, you will not have been without news from me for such a very long time. I am afraid however that it is too late to write it all on the typewriter, which [is] too bad, since I cannot cram as much in by hand of course.

On the other hand, it looks as if there is [not] much news to tell you after my last letter to Gerrit, only that Paul and Selma arrived here safely, and that I was happy that I could welcome them and could help make them as comfortable as possible right away.

After two weeks' silence I finally received Gerrit's letter with the news of their coming on Monday evening, just in time for me to be present at their arrival and to be able to assist them as much as possible. Luckily I have been partially successful in helping them in many respects. It just so happened that a bunk below mine had been vacated, which

164   Signs of Life

I managed to reserve for Selma immediately, so that we are together as often as my work allows, and I must say that I find their company as pleasant and congenial as in the good old days. The two of them had a good night's sleep, and their appetite is as good as mine. They have been very lucky with the food the first few days, for we had sauerkraut and potatoes yesterday and pea soup today, both just about the most glamorous items on the menu.

You must of course send some sausage, which they love, as you know, and I also count on your sending butter and bread as soon as possible, especially butter which Paul badly needs because of his stomach. Also a jar of jam at least once a week, and some black bread and cheese. I am sure Gerrit will be willing to help you get and package these items. Father can take care of the mailing himself. Please do not forget to include a piece of roasted meat as often as possible, preferably veal, as it keeps better and stays fresher in the warmer weather. This reminds me, please tell Gerrit that parcels containing roasted meat do better if sent by first class mail as registered parcel post (maximum weight 2 kilograms). That goes faster than through the Jewish Council, although they do very well by me otherwise, I must say. But since they are so busy, there sometimes is a day's delay in the delivery, which is just long enough for the meat to be on the verge of spoiling when we get it.

I understand that it was no trivial matter for the two of you that Selma and Paul had to leave after all, but we shall try to make life here as pleasant for them as possible. Fortunately the weather is beautiful and sunny again these last few days, and not so windy, which makes the place look less somber right away.

It is a terrible shame and also incredibly dumb that they did not bring any official papers proving that Lotte is living in Palestine, for that would probably have made things easier for them here. I am convinced that Lotte must have finished her studies by now, and that she has resumed her job as an X-ray technician in the hospital on Mount

Carmel, next door to which they had been living recently. Perhaps Gerrit can talk this matter over with Dr. Albersheim of the emigration department at the Jewish Council. We also talked it over with Heidenheimer, who wrote about it to the Jewish Council.

I also urgently request that you send two excellent thick blankets for Selma and Paul right away and with the utmost speed, the best ones you have, not those thin summer blankets, because otherwise it will be much too cold for them here. Fortunately I had an extra blanket for them, and I could borrow another one from a friend, otherwise it would have been hopeless. If you need more blankets yourselves, Gerrit can certainly spare a few!!!

[Hand-written addition]

In addition, they really need bowls to eat from and a couple of mugs (unbreakable). They only brought some small flat plates from which they really cannot eat soup or mashed food! Perhaps Gerrit can manage to find some canteens for them too! As far as the [illegible] declaration is concerned, I'll give you the following data: Charlotte Edith Wallman born 8.26.06. Harry Rosenthal, May 3, approx. 1895. Married 2.27.1930 in Tel Aviv. Address: Beit Markus, Mount Carmel Road next to "ESRA" Hospital (for Women). Please have Father or Gait arrange that with Dr. Albersheim right away; perhaps you can locate some proof of it somewhere if they do not want to take your word for it. Getting rid of all that evidence was the dumbest move ever.

I really hope that Gerrit has recovered fully and that he is not feeling too weak from lying in bed all that time. I will be very happy if he can visit here again really soon, so we can have an opportunity to talk together quietly, even though that is pretty hard to do here. At the moment I am sitting in the barrack finishing this letter, and it is unbelievably hard to find a quiet spot for writing, so I won't write a great deal more.

Otto dropped over tonight for a chat, and Sam dropped in to see him too. I only hope that you will be able to send us good news, because we are always very happy to hear from you. Even if you don't have much to report, your letters are always most welcome.

I have a few more messages for Gerrit, namely would he please send the candy promised to Ro and I also have not heard any more about the backpack that was ordered.

I am in great need of the clean laundry and I hope that you will have shipped it out already by the time this letter arrives. I hope you will send a lot of rusks and biscuits for Paul, because he really needs those. Dear Mother, please remember that all other things are totally unimportant in these times: here we do not dust the floors everyday either, and yet we stay in good health; but nutrition *is* very important. Also please send some apples and cucumbers some time. I would also like to have some more of that "old-fashioned brand" tomato juice; also the jam bucket is actually somewhat too small, so perhaps you could get me a larger one sometime.

Today many of Daan's roommates arrived, and I was very relieved to see that he was not among them. I find that a very good sign and I hope that he will soon be fully recovered at long last. Please give my kindest regards to Bé and Loutje and if I ever have a minute I shall certainly try to write them again. How is Arthur (Buby)? It seems that he is still very much attracted to the theater, as I heard from his parents! Well, my dears, I am really going to end this; otherwise the letter will definitely not make this mail pick-up. I hope that you will make do with this rambling letter for today, and I send you my warmest thoughts and lots of kisses, and embrace you warmly in my thoughts.

Hilde

Please have Gerrit read this letter right away and give him lots of kisses from me!

Please send all items requested for Paul and Selma soon and in generous quantities.

Otto Sluizer, Hilde's brother.

Hilde and Gerrit on the tennis court, before the war.

Signs of Life

A class of Jewish children, all wearing the Jewish star in accordance with Nazi regulations. Yoka sits in the second row, second from right, squinting against the sun.

1943

171

LETTERS FROM WESTERBORK OCTOBER 1943 TO FEBRUARY 1944

Hilde with her father on holiday, 1930s.

Introduction
To the Letters
To Corrie van Abs

The break in the letters from Westerbork after April 1943 can be explained by a series of arrests and releases. According to Gerrit's letter of July 1945, Hilde was released in June 1943 because of his job at the Jewish Council. Ten days later, however, she was arrested again, and this time Gerrit was also sent to Westerbork. Gerrit was freed after two weeks and Hilde was released for the second time in September. This time her release lasted barely a week, as on Wednesday, September 29, 1943, all the Jews left in Amsterdam were rounded up and transported to the camp. Gerrit escaped only because he happened to be out of town for the day.

The letters resume shortly thereafter, in October. They are now handwritten rather than typed because Hilde had lost her secretarial job and no longer had access to a typewriter. Hilde's mood has also changed. The energy and optimism of the earlier letters are much less evident. She is more pessimistic and feels deportation is inevitable as she sees train after train departing with inexorable regularity every

1944   175

Tuesday for parts and fates unknown. At one point she sarcastically refers to her own expected deportation as "a little detour." Her worries are compounded by her concern for her elderly parents and parents-in-law who are now also in the camp.

The first three letters from this period are written to Corrie van Abs, a Gentile friend from Hilversum. In the first letter, when Hilde refers to Gerrit who can no longer write because he has gone into hiding, she says, "His health leaves nothing to be desired"; she means that he is in a safe place. As we see in the very next sentence, however, his actual physical health is not as good.

Clearly Corrie is a very reliable and helpful friend; Hilde mentions her often in other letters. Not only does she write regularly, but she also sends much needed parcels. Evidently, she knows where things are and Hilde frequently asks her to find articles of clothing and other items and send them to Westerbork. Corrie also sends food, especially apples, and even such basic essentials as toilet paper and sanitary napkins. The survival of the inmates of camps such as Westerbork depended on the care and generosity of people like Corrie van Abs and her sons, Robbert and Arnout.

Another such person was Lé Cohen, to whom Hilde refers here as "my faithful friend in Overveen." We know very little about Lé. A teacher of geography at the gymnasium in Overveen, and a Jew, he managed to live openly during the war years with false identity papers. He worked tirelessly for the underground, doing anything and everything he could. Among other things, he arranged hiding places for fellow Jews, sheltered people in his own home, and was a contact for smuggled messages. It is evident that Hilde and Gerrit, too, benefited from his great courage.

[Sunday, October 17, 1943]

Dear Corrie,

Even though the message I received from you via various detours was rather vague, still it was news from the outside world, which pleased me very much.

Of course I would love to get a letter from you sometime, for mail is what we long for most here, at least I do, the more so now that Gerrit is not in a position to write anymore.

I heard to my great joy that his health leaves nothing to be desired, knock on wood!! I just hope that his stomach complaints will also disappear now that he is getting more rest. My friend told me that you had been at our door; you must have been shocked when no one answered. Well, I must confess that it was not a pleasant experience on Wednesday morning to be so rudely awakened and forced to take this trip against my will for the third time. The shock was so intense that I have not got over it yet, but time will heal this wound too, and fortunately I still have many reasons to be very, very grateful. Of course it is no small matter to be treated in this way twice in so short a period, and to tell you the truth I had not expected it to happen so soon after my second release; that may be the reason why I was so deeply shaken this time. Moreover, this time my in-laws and my own parents did not escape their clutches either! So that meant the end of everything and the irrevocable loss of many dear and irreplaceable memories. My in-laws were incredibly brave and kept their composure throughout, which undoubtedly made things easier for me at the time.

I also got the message that you sent me a package, but I have to tell you that to date, Sunday, October 17th, I have not received anything from you, and as far as I can check here, no package for me or my brother has arrived here that we haven't received. So, if you really sent something already, I ask you urgently to have it traced right away, since it did not arrive here. Please also let me know name of addressee and date sent, then I can try once more to trace it here. I hope it is still forthcoming, or traceable, for it would be a great pity if it has got lost. It might have contained the gloves and stockings I requested and I really need those desperately, for in the rush I forgot to pack the stockings I had in Amsterdam. So here's hoping that you haven't sent them yet or if you have, that you will send me another set as soon as possible. Could you also get me a pair of sheep's wool mittens? In case you cannot lend me the money until my return, payment may be arranged via our friends the Br[andt]s.

I also urgently need a package of cotton and sanitary napkins. I would also like to have the red shoes if you can get them for me. But don't make your parcels too large, because of the chance of one getting lost, and have them mailed in *Amsterdam*, since they may *not* be distributed to us otherwise, unless you send it as *first class mail* (maximum weight 2 kilograms). Mailing in Amsterdam is always *safer* however. The Jewish Council still seems to be handling parcels too.

Please be sure to send me *candles*, and matches and toilet paper. Mr. Br[andt] can help with this too and it is possible that he himself has sent me these things in the meantime. I am back in number 68 again. Hilde V.S.28-11-09. I have no urgent need for food at the moment, although I have received only one package so far, and that was two weeks ago.

If you should happen to come across a laying hen somewhere, however, I would love to have some eggs, especially since they provide such excellent nutrition, as does cheese, and of course fruit is always very welcome, and you, dear Corrie, always used to have such good sources for fruit.

Well my dear, I won't overload you with requests and assignments, only this one request that you write me very soon, which is something that you may also ask the other girls to do some time. Please give them my best regards. I hope that your two gentlemen are all right too and that you have no special difficulties in that respect.

Please write me soon, especially since the situation is so uncertain now that there is a chance that otherwise your letter will not reach me anymore. Please do not forget to make thorough inquiries after the parcel, if you did send it, and to tell me about it in detail especially to whom and to what barrack you had addressed it.

Much love and kindest regards, especially to your sons, too, and a hug for you from your

Hilde

Dear Corrie,

I was terribly happy to get a long letter from you at last and I was very happy with the parcel too. Of course everything was very useful; the mittens are terrific and the shoes are very welcome, as is the rest of the contents.

I'll continue in pencil, as my pen is giving out. From your letter I read that you sent a large package to Otto right after our departure. Did you remember that he lived in barrack 69? Unfortunately, we never received it, and as far as I could find out after thorough sleuthing here, it never did arrive at the camp.

Since they check very carefully, I cannot imagine that it would have disappeared here, so I ask you urgently to make thorough inquiries about it right away. I am afraid however that an investigation will not do much good anymore. What a pity about the precious contents. Still, we don't have more than a moment to spare here to mourn such trifles, as we have no time to dwell longer than that on any one thing in this maelstrom. The package with the shoes arrived promptly and in good condition and yesterday I received another parcel of delicious apples from you, for which I am extremely grateful. Obviously, mailing them as first class parcel post works well, but I still would advise you to mail them from Amsterdam, for you never know what changes they may make in the regulations here, and parcels from Amsterdam are always delivered while parcels mailed in the country are often confiscated. Since Rob happens to pass through the Central Station every day anyway, it wouldn't be any trouble for him to put them in the mail there. And in the future, better not send packages that are too large, because they may get lost.

Yes, I can imagine how upset you were to hear that I was forced to end my vacation after no more than ten days, and it is strange that we did not see each other at the station in Amersfoort on that fateful Wednesday, because I was also looking out for friends in Hilversum and Amersfoort of course. It was a terrible shock for me too, to be chased from my home again after such a short stay in Amsterdam, for, although I should have known better, I still hoped that they would leave me alone for a little while after having released me for a second time. So I still haven't quite got over the shock, and I often feel very depressed. But I do have to get through this and after all I have very many reasons to be infinitely grateful, which I never forget. Still, you should write me again soon, for getting mail is the most wonderful thing, even though it also makes me sad and nostalgic. Besides your letter, I have unfortunately received only one other letter, from my faithful friend in Overveen.

How are the Brandts? I am surprised that I haven't heard anything from them in all this time, and I hope there is no special reason for that. I have to stop now, and hope to hear from you again soon.

Are you all right, and how are your sons? Also give my best regards to the girls, please, and my warmest thoughts and a kiss to you from your grateful

Hilde

[Additions in the margins]

Fortunately, my father and mother-in-law are taking this very well indeed. My own parents are not doing so well. Mother has had dysentery for three weeks and is in the hospital. I am happy to report however that her condition is improving now. Father is very much bothered by arthritis!

Please write again soon. Don't forget to find out about the Brandts.

[Middle of November, 1943]

Dear Corrie,

In a spare moment, while I am sitting in the dental clinic waiting my turn, I want to start a letter to you, hoping you will receive it in good health.

I was very happy with your wonderful long letter, and I thank you very much for it. It's wonderful to get some news from the outside world for a change, even though the news is not always good and even though it makes me all the more nostalgic for a life with at least a semblance of normalcy. Imagine us here in these drafty, damp barracks virtually without heat in the middle of November!

Even though there are two puny little potbellied stoves in a space 40 x 160 feet, the stoker doesn't know what he is doing and there is practically no kindling to start the fire, so as late as eleven o'clock this morning there was still no trace of heat to be felt, even if you were right on top of the stove. While this is no fun for us, imagine the plight of mothers with sick children or, like a friend of ours, with a four-week-old baby.

It is really surprising that there are not many more sick people here, especially since the washroom is entirely without heat and we have to stand on a sopping wet, muddy cement floor, so that the cold comes up through our feet. And with our rich diet we obviously have terrific protection against the dampness and cold! For lack of a stiff drink [to warm the blood], I have taken to wearing wooden shoes in order to keep my feet at least reasonably warm, and this seems to work. You should see me clumping around like a real Dutch farmer's wife. But this way I keep my feet dry even in the rain and mud of the past few weeks, and I save my shoes as well.

Time passes slowly and disconsolately, and the end of this misery is not yet in sight, despite the assertions of those insane enough to be optimistic even now. Everyone here is impatient, but much good that does. The only bright spots, aside from the few letters I receive, are the packages I get: besides yours, so far just two from our friend in Overveen. I'll have to start doing something about making better arrangements to receive food, for I am getting to the end of the ration cards I brought along and there is no other way to get additional food. After all, as long as it is not absolutely necessary, I have no desire to starve quite yet. After reading these tales of woe, you can imagine how very much your shipments please me; they always arrive promptly, except for one small parcel which was under two kilograms but not sent first class and therefore confiscated. It was the next to last package, containing apples meant for me. However, since I was alerted right away to the fact that the parcel had been confiscated and since I could prove that I rarely get anything sent, I did get compensated. Actually it is also against the regulations to include notes even in the parcels sent first class; that is not a regulation of the Postal Service but of the authorities here. I have received all of your notes that you included, however, but it would be better to send them separately.

I also received the apples for my parents-in-law right away and passed them on. They were very grateful and have probably already written to thank you. They are in barrack 62, but you can also continue to send things to me, if there is anything more to send, that is.

Please don't complain that you have to spend so much time traveling. Don't forget that at least you are doing it of your own volition. If you had lived in my circumstances for a year, with the weekly fear of an involuntary trip, you would begin to understand the value of your freedom, all your forced voluntary traveling included.

We've had a few weeks' respite now, at a price though: very serious illnesses, such as diphtheria, hepatitis and, worst of all, close to thirty cases of polio, although fortunately without very serious consequences so far. But in spite of all this, another transport of a thousand people has unexpectedly been scheduled again for this Tuesday. I am still exempt for the time being and hope to remain so for a while longer, but even so the suffering is once again indescribable.

You may begin to understand that under the circumstances we do not consider the loss of a wrist watch a disaster. I understand that it was sad for you, but to us it means less than nothing. Keep in mind how we had to leave our homes at a moment's notice, being allowed to take only what we could carry. Not only [did we lose] furniture and other valuables, which by the way will certainly be impossible to replace in the first few years, but also all the memories attached to them. The worst thing for me was that when I returned here the third time I forgot to take an enamel dish and a little cooking pot. But I have gotten over that too. I borrow one from my aunt and uncle Wallman. When we left, my mother-in-law forgot to take her back pack containing all her warm clothes and underwear. Can you imagine what that means in our present situation!! So stop grieving for your wrist watch, it will certainly be replaceable; I shall be very happy to buy you one if only one tenth of all the rest will turn out all right. First, let us hope that we'll all be reunited in good health and freedom, that is if this beastliness does not go on so long that all our energy and spirits are broken.

In the meantime it is beginning to look as if we'll first have to make a little detour. Before that time I had better get some more provisions I think, in order to have some food at least for the trip, if it should come to that. Would you kindly discuss this with our friends the Brandts who have to talk this over with Jan Barens. Right now I would need at least one or two loaves of bread and a pound of butter every week, especially since my aunt and uncle and also my brother hardly get anything, so that we all share with my parents who are being fairly well supplied so far.

I am pretty sure that Aukje has some jam left or otherwise the Br[andt]s may still be able to get some. What about cans of fruit and vegetables? Is any of that stock left? I also would like to have some calcium lactate, about half a pound (best stored in a jam jar), two bottles of aspirin, a roll of adhesive tape and some type of vitamin tablets, Dumine [?] tablets as a last resort, although I do not think those are very potent.

If there are any two-pound cans of butter left, please send the *unopened* one, as it has to keep.

If you go to the "Vergulde Gaper" pharmacy in the Kerkstraat for the medicines, and tell them that it is for me, I am sure that he will take very good care of you. I am also in great need of a bottle of ink, a handy traveling bottle please, if possible. Also some tubes of toothpaste, please.

Would it be possible to get hold of a canteen or enamel workman's canteen from someone or other, because my canteen was also left at home, together with my eating dish. And if you have a couple of old dishes, plain crockery if you have no enamel ones (soup bowls, because dinner plates are useless here), please include them.

Then I would very much like to have my very old light blue sweat suit. It was stored in a hat box, on top of the linen cupboard, and I would like to have it here to wear at night over my nightgown. Please launder it first. I am sure Br[andt] can find it. I had asked him about it before and am very surprised that I never heard from him. What on earth might be the reason? I was happy to hear at any rate that everything seems to be all right with him so far, but I would certainly like to have some sign of life from him personally.

I got your greetings the other day from the meeting at the station in Amersfoort, and I learned the fate of my first parcel. In the meantime I also received the latest parcel with the delicious fondant candy, and I really want to thank you. It was a wonderful treat, especially because it is impossible to get hold of anything like that here. It was immediately consumed with the help of my aunt and uncle and other interested parties, for almost everything is shared here, now that all cupboards are equally bare because of the scarcity of parcels. Anyway, in the event of a further journey we'd have to do without altogether, so we might as well get used to it now.

[Additions in the margins]

Well my dear, I am ending here and I will be awfully happy to hear from you again soon.

Lots of love and warm regards, especially to the sons too! A kiss for you from your

Hilde

Introduction
To Letters Starting
November 28, 1943

The following letter is the first one Hilde writes to Gerrit after he has gone into hiding. Two months have already passed since September 29, when she arrived in Westerbork for the last time. Like so many others, her overriding concern now is to remain in the camp as long as possible. At least in Westerbork she knows what she is up against, whereas who knows what lies ahead at the other end of the train trip.

In order to avoid deportation, inmates tried to get their names on lists which supposedly guaranteed exemption. Rumors ran rampant through the camp as to which list was the best. Several of these lists are mentioned by Hilde in this and subsequent letters. The various lists, such as the Calmeyer list and the Weinreb list are explained in detail in the Foreword to this book.

The Germans also thought up exemption categories such as the "blue Z" and the "green Z" mentioned by Hilde. The categories and the exemptions were frequently changed.

At one time a blue Z was a privileged stamp for, among others, members of the Jewish Council. These and countless other lists and stamps, which supposedly offered protection against deportation, all proved to be futile and worthless. In the end the Nazis meant to deport everyone.

Hilde writes about another designation which was to be avoided at all costs. This was the infamous "S" stamp which stood for "Straf" meaning punishment. Those receiving this stamp, such as the wife of Dr. K. and Mrs. Weismann and others mentioned by Hilde, were confined to the punishment barracks, literally a prison within a prison, because they were considered to be trouble makers by their Nazi wardens. Usually, confinement to the punishment barracks meant deportation on the very next transport.

One possible way out of the camp was to try to make an escape, something Gerrit repeatedly urges Hilde to do. The prospect of an escape is discussed several times in this and the next two letters to Gerrit. Hilde writes about a friend who is "leaving" and, in a subsequent letter, about a friend who is "planning to play Saint Nicolas," an obvious euphemism for someone who is trying to arrange an escape for her. The Dutch holiday of Saint Nicolas falls on December 5, therefore it would hardly be a likely topic for discussion in early January. Saint Nicolas traditionally comes at night, plays tricks and brings surprises. Not only was this terribly risky, but Hilde is unable to accept the "decidedly immoral aspect of it," the immediate deportation of her relatives and barrack mates. Once other family members have left, she assures Gerrit, she will attempt an escape.

Unfortunately, events do not go the way Hilde envisions. Sometime in early December 1943, Hilde's situation takes another turn for the worse: she becomes ill with hepatitis. Her last letters are all written from her hospital bed. In the past, confinement to the camp hospital was considered to be a stroke of good luck. It meant that one was exempted from going on transport—the Jewish doctors regularly declared patients "unfit to travel." Thus, in spite of her illness, Hilde still feels relatively, though only temporarily, safe.

Gerrit managed to have food packages sent again from his farm hide-out in Friesland. Previously Gerrit had arranged through his contact, Jan Barens, to send provisions to the camp. Jan had then made arrangements with someone else, Willem Siemons (Siem), to take on this responsibility. As it turned out, though, Siemons never sent any packages. When Gerrit discovered this, he was furious and it took some time before he was able to make an alternative arrangement. It was imperative to send these food parcels, since the camp food was totally inadequate. When the war ended, Siem and Gerrit were reconciled. Evidently Siem had misunderstood his task. As Gerrit writes in his letter of July 1945, he hired Siem, a lawyer, to work with him again in his business.

Hilde starts her last letter on January 12, the day after the departure of her brother and her aunt and uncle, but there is an interruption and she does not resume writing until the end of the month, more than two weeks later. More often now she identifies people by an initial or by a cautious description in order to protect them should the letters ever fall into the wrong hands. This, however, is not the reason why she refers to herself as "Mouse." "Mouse" was Gerrit's pet name for her.

The last section of this long letter, dated January 31, expresses her extreme anxiety over the status of the various family members still left in Westerbork. Hilde's frustration at not being able to do more to protect them as she lies confined to her bed is clearly evident.

Hilde's note to her father, scribbled in haste and desperation on the eve of her deportation, is indescribably painful. It is unbearable to try to imagine her state of mind during those last few hours. This note, written in pencil, carefully folded, with the lower left-hand corner torn off, survived somehow in our grandfather David's pocket throughout the fifteen months he was imprisoned in

Theresienstadt. It is the last sign of life from Hilde before she was killed in Auschwitz.

View of Westerbork with railroad on the left.

1944

[November 28, 1943]

Dear Gerrit,

As you can imagine, I was very happy to get a sign of life directly from you, and although I had been waiting for it for ages, it still took me by surprise.

Although I'm not sure whether this letter will reach you, I want to use the afternoon of my birthday to write to you all the same, so I have installed myself on my third floor perch high above the swirling Sunday afternoon crowd. I quickly found out about your situation through your message via Bernard Denneboom, and as you may have heard from others in the meantime, I am totally and entirely content with it! I just hope that you're doing all right and I do believe that you will make it through all this; your letter also reassured me in this respect.

Well, it was no fun to be woken up at about 8 a.m. on Wednesday morning by what sounded like a fire alarm; since I had been home scarcely ten days, it was a terrible shock to me. It took me weeks to get over it, especially the realization that this was irrevocably the end, and also the fact that this time our parents would not escape either. Add to that your absence, and consequently the realization that I had to save what little I could save for you as well.

Fortunately I heard from Snijders in the meantime that he did everything I had asked him to do, and I assume that Jack forwarded the parcels to you. The only thing I forgot to take for you was a winter coat, and several less important items such as food bowls, saucepans, canteen, etc. which I have already stopped grieving about.

The realization that this place, or perhaps even another one, unknown as yet, would be my winter quarters, was also a deeply depressing prospect, but now that the shortest day of the year is almost upon us again, and some people are naively optimistic, I see things in a somewhat lighter vein again too. Your parents, as well as mine, are doing fairly well. Your parents are adjusting much better than mine and fortunately remain in good health and spirits. It is too bad that they get so little mail and skimpy parcels, but we share what we have.

The care I get is no care at all, because except for a few shipments of apples from Corrie and some thoughtful packages from our dear Lé, I have only received two parcels from the O.S. I happened to have my new ration card with me though, and moreover Father is supplied so generously that all of us, Otto, Paul and Selma included, can share in it. Now that my ration cards are all used up, I asked Lé to contact Jan and Jack after all, but there really is no need for you to worry! For you know my feelings about food, it still means very little to me. But it would be nice to get rid of the blah taste in my mouth and to have something tasty for a change.

Not getting any letters is much harder for me to bear, and if I do get one every now and then, it usually contains nothing but vague generalities and no information at all about the specific things I am so very eager to hear about. Lé is very good and does what he can and you know how difficult it is to get hold of Jack, since he is almost always "on the road." I would rather not write directly to Jack or Jan. I got a letter from Thily Siemons once, a real specimen of shallow claptrap. One thing is clear now: I certainly had them pegged right! The Mays do not get anything anymore now that they have to depend on their good care, and I suspect that it will be the same story for Kee's sister-in-law and the old Broekman couple. But again, it is of no consequence whatsoever!

It is probably much more interesting for you to know that your parents as well as mine are safe for the time being on their 120. My own situation was very tenuous at first, and I was quite uneasy about it, with the prospect of having to pay the price after all. But after two weeks I was exempted once more "until reunited with spouse," and I have a blue "Z" again. So you see what a good thing it is that you are not here, even though there is no telling yet how the situation will develop of course.

Philipson is still here, probably under someone's protection; and Schuit has an exemption through his wife's working at the Herzberg workshop. Sarlui has a green "Z" through the mattress factory. Zeelander left and unfortunately so did Henri Anholt last time. I was very sad about that, for his own sake in the first place, but also for mine, for he was one of the very few pillars of my weak support system here.

Now our friend is leaving too. Although I rarely saw him, his presence here used to give me some security all the same. His plan does not appeal to me for many reasons; and apart from the decidedly immoral aspect of it, which I really cannot take lightly, his plan seems impracticable to me. Perhaps a better opportunity will present itself some time.

Bernhard is very nice to me; from time to time we eat together, but I do not see him very often either. Still he is really and truly concerned about me. I also spend time every now and then with Jetty Lissauer and Flatow and the girls, but due to that old affair Jessie is unfortunately gone, and Boris, the old rascal, has come off without a scratch. So you see how unexpectedly a penny can roll sometimes.

Otto is doing quite well and has totally recovered from his operation; he is happy to have it over with. My mother has been suffering from very bad diarrhea which even put her in the hospital for three weeks; the beneficial side effect was a good rest. As far as my job is concerned, I am doing child care in #68 again, but not always with a great deal of enthusiasm. With a view to greater protection I may try to be reassigned to the sewing workshop, but as you know my interest in working is not very great here, also because the protection it offers is questionable at best. Well, I suppose we'll manage to survive somehow.

Here is another tidbit for you: your old friend Lex got married here this past week, and there was a very beautiful and solemn *chupah* with many of the big wheels from the Jewish C.B. in attendance.

I would like to know what your ideas are about the "Weinreb Exchange." There may be a chance for us to get onto that list too. Perhaps you are not informed on the subject, but there is a new Weinreb list for legal emigration to Portugal and one thousand people from Holland will be eligible. People's faith in this enterprise varies, and I myself really do not know what to make of it. I'll write to Siem about it at any rate, and perhaps Mo could also look into it sometime. People with approved Palestine-Exchange papers or of foreign nationality are not eligible.

The big problem for me is of course that I cannot apply for it here, as I cannot give your address. I'll also try to sound out Hans Ott. on this matter, which I have been unable to do for the past few days because I was running a bit of a temperature: probably a cold, but it wasn't anything serious and has almost disappeared by now.

There is still another possible option, namely the ancestry business of Berta and Dé. If that turns out well, they would have excellent prospects of course, and Otto would then automatically also be in good shape. That would leave me out in the cold, unless we could find someone who would testify that Jan Dank[1] for instance was your father. If the matter works out for my parents, that ought to work too, and it should be possible to find people willing to do that. I broached the subject with your mother a few days ago, but she looked extremely doubtful and did not seem to understand what it was all about. My father's counsel, Mr.

Mehring, and Atty. de Kort are quite optimistic and are sure it will work. If it does work, I am sure it will surpass even your wildest gumshoe fantasies! I hope that you or otherwise Jack will soon be able to send me some news and to tell me what you think of these matters. Do you see Jack often?

Our friend brought me a splendid Edam cheese, 40 percent fat; of course I'll give your parents a big chunk. I definitely won't say anything about your letter though, because you know how that will make them prod and question, so I'd rather leave them in the dark. You know that otherwise I would not have a quiet moment, but this way they are not aware that there is any news.

Our return here, especially mine, was cause for a great deal of commotion of course, and when our train entered the station, loud and spirited comments were flying back and forth. Otto was in the hospital at the time, as you know, but his friends Herman, Paul and Frits came to welcome and assist me right away.

My first impulse was to try and leave again by the same train, and perhaps I should really have tried it, but I didn't; which I may come to regret, who is to say! No one knew the details of your situation, until Floortje finally told me the whole story. If you had asked me about it, I would have given you the exact same advice. Floor and I had, after all, talked about these things often in our late night conversations so that she knew exactly how I feel about this. Of course it was too bad that you were not at home, but that could not be helped.

I am happy to hear that you are feeling well, but I do object to your putting on weight. The main thing though is that your stomach is behaving itself, and I fervently hope that it will continue to do so.

I want to assure you once more that you do not have to worry about us, and that we are none the worse for your absence; on the contrary, as I wrote to you before, I even got an exemption for that reason! I picked up the blankets at

Horowitz's and I gave them to your parents, who had brought only one big blanket each. I also got them decent new pillows from the Stroma.

I am pleased that you managed to do something special for the 16th [Yoka's ninth birthday] after all. The poem was a beauty too, as usual. I hope she also received the brooch; I had given it to our faithful Anholt upon our departure, but I haven't heard if she got it and if Fransje got hers. No sign from Anholt after that, unfortunately. I also don't know if the winter coat for Yoka which I asked him to drop off at the Swaan's at #12 around the corner got to its destination.

[Additions in the margins]

Perhaps you could ask Jack about these things some time. Dear Gerrit I am stopping now, even though I could write many more pages, but my pen is giving me no end of trouble.

Well, my dear Gait, stay well and keep up your courage. Don't worry, it doesn't do any good any way! I send you many, many kisses in my thoughts.

Yours, Hilde

Let me hear from you soon, very soon if possible!

I talked to the Zwaaps several times and they are always very cordial and invite me to visit them. I also visit Asch quite often. She was quite upset though when she found out that her precious fur wrap was gone.

On November 1st Selma and Paul had their fortieth wedding anniversary and we managed to put together a pleasant little dinner with chicken soup for the occasion! Asch gave us the use of her room, so it got to be quite a nice affair, considering the circumstances.

To: Mr. and Mrs. J.G. van de Beek
288 Driebergenstraat
Den Haag

From: H. Verdoner-Sluizer
Barrack 83
Born: 11-28-09
Camp Westerbork
Hooghalen Oost

Camp Westerbork
Hooghalen Oost
January 1, 1944

Dear Grada and Hans,

This will probably be quite a surprise getting a sign of life from me once again, but I do not get a chance to write very often of course. Today, at the beginning of the new year, I really wanted to let you know that my thoughts are with you very, very often.

I heard that you had an addition to the family around August, and although I am very late congratulating you, I am sure I do not have to tell you how very, very happy I am for you. Your son must be quite a gentleman by now, and I can imagine what a source of joy and pleasure he is to you.

How are your parents? Please give them my best, and I also would like to know if you ever see Toos these days, or hear from her. As luck would have it, the visit which she had planned to pay us during my short stay in Amsterdam did not work out. We were terribly sorry about that, and in the meantime she probably had an addition to the family too. I really hope that all went smoothly.

Please reply in detail some time on the attached reply form. If you would like more information about me, you might contact Lé Cohen, our friend from Overveen, some time. I am reasonably well at the moment, but for the fact that I have hepatitis; this too will pass, however. Fortunately I feel well in spite of it.

Warmest regards and best wishes from

your H.V.S.

[This is the only letter written on official camp stationery. Printed on the form: "Write only on the lines!" (in German), and in the appropriate space "Checked" (also in German) was stamped by a censor.]

[Early January, 1944]

My Dear Gait,

What excitement last night, as you can imagine! I was really exhausted after reading and devouring it all, and also from the emotional upheaval of getting so much news so suddenly, and I was especially happy that it was all—knock on wood—such good news.

Since I was a bit tired yesterday, I had actually started my letter too late, so that I ran out of time and had to hand it in unfinished. But I had already touched upon the most important points, so you could fill in a proper ending yourself.

Today was visiting day, so again I could not really start my letter until after six o'clock. Then I can write without interruptions. You were hospitalized yourself once, so you know that on a huge ward like mine a patient is kept busy from 5 a.m. on, with the result that I doze off every now and then, especially since hepatitis tends to make one very drowsy. You really and truly do not have to worry about me in any way though, because I really feel fine, and bed rest will take care of it.

We do not get any medication here; anyway I don't know if there are any known remedies for this disease besides consuming a lot of sugar, which is why all patients receive half a pound of sugar and half a pound of jam apiece every week. In addition, I eat toast, and at noon a tiny serving of baby food. I mix the sugar into sugar water in order to consume a sizable quantity of fluids without having to drink tap water all the time. I've been trying to get soda water for as long as I've been down with this, but even with Hermine's help, unsuccessfully so far.

Of course I was delighted to hear that all is going well with you and that you feel well. Is your stomach not bothering you anymore and can you eat everything that is served? And how about smoking??? The fact that you get so much exercise and fresh air is wonderful too. You don't know how lucky you are, for you cannot imagine how I, fresh-air and open-window fiend that I am, suffer here in a ward with more than a hundred patients, bedpans, etc., where howls go up from all sides whenever a window is opened so much as a crack. I find that worse than the worst pain. I think you can imagine the situation. And to think that visitors always tell me that our ward is quite bearable compared to the others; that is my doing of course. During nap time in the afternoon I always bribe some nurses to open a couple of windows for a half hour or so, and then I dare breathe again.

Now I'll start responding from memory to your letter, and if there is enough time I'll reread the letter later. But first let me thank you very much on behalf of *all* of us for all the things you sent and which *all* were very happy to have; we'll toast the sender when we eat them. Everyone was notably short of butter, and since I don't need any just now, I gave my package to Selma who can make better use of it, for with my hepatitis I must go very easy on butter at the moment.

I nibbled a piece of the meat, which was delicious, but the fat part is too rich for me now so I gave it to my parents who thank you most kindly for it and also for the other delicacies. From the few words which your mother added to this letter when she visited me this afternoon, you can tell how very excited she was. As I didn't know whether I'd have another way to get a letter to you, I had Mother write that note here, but I did tell her to write another letter at her leisure in case another opportunity presents itself.

I agree one hundred percent with Mother's opening phrase, and you'll have to remember always that you yourself and also W. must keep practicing extreme caution for the sake of all concerned and especially in order not to compromise F.

Mother didn't want to bother you with requests but she had told me earlier that she would really like to have some more towels and perhaps two pillowcases and also a little saucepan to cook something in every now and then. Perhaps this can be arranged for them, especially since I believe parcels not containing edible goods may still be sent in the old way, via the Jewish Council.

Would it be possible to retrieve some things from Mother's laundry man? Right before our departure, on September 26, if I'm not mistaken, he had picked up a big load of laundry, and we had someone make inquiries, but never heard any more about it. His address is: Ettema's Apeldoornsche Waschverzending, Uithoornstraat, Amsterdam. If it is possible to pry the laundry loose from him, perhaps it could be sent here in several medium-sized shipments. Whatever we don't need ourselves we can use to help out a great many others.

I myself do not need a thing, but fruit of course would be very welcome, and I would like some good cough drops, licorice or eucalyptus candies or something like that if you can manage to get hold of those, for I have a persistent dry cough which is keeping me awake at night and the doctor has not come up with a remedy yet. Well, that's really all I have to tell about me.

I was overjoyed to get the news about the trio and the delightful letter from Yoka. How much longer?

At any rate I am terribly grateful for everything and I do want to say most emphatically that you may never ever reproach Jan with anything, as if he had committed the most awful deed. We should not bear him a grudge for the fact that he let Siem take charge of the sending of packages without checking whether they were actually being sent, for who would have guessed that Siem would be such a miserable clod, except for me who has always had the arrogance to think so! It appears that I have always had his number, and of others as well. So it was also his fault that you weren't at home anymore! Well, it's water under the bridge now and there is no sense in grieving about it any longer. It is also not to M[o] W[olff]'s credit that he selects such co-workers and then holds on to them. You certainly won't agree with this opinion of mine, but I didn't just arrive at it!

I shall have to be more concise in order to deal with everything. First, I want to tell you that the Callmeyer thing is not working out after all for Bertha and Dé, mostly because the procedure was started a year too late; so you can drop that entirely, and as far as the Weinreb list is concerned, I'm not putting any bets on that one either. So let's just roll along and see what happens. Anyway, I must get better first and that will certainly take several more weeks.

I think your disappointment with Bernhard is utterly unfounded. His papers were in perfectly good order and the only thing that thwarted our plans was the total quarantine. He himself had after all not had a leave for two months and got it very unexpectedly in the middle of December through the untiring efforts of our boss. He was always extremely helpful, warm, and concerned about me. I cannot put it any other way, and I consider him totally and entirely trustworthy.

My darling I must stop now but shall start another letter tomorrow in hopes that it will be picked up. I was quite surprised to hear that you were already counting so firmly on my arrival, whereas you are familiar enough with the circumstances here. I am very sorry that you were so disappointed at my not coming.

Well dear Gait, keep well, give my best regards to *all* and thank everyone from all of us. Stay well and do take care.

Lots of love and my warmest embrace [scrawl]

If another opportunity should arise, please include something for the railway cars!!! S.z.z. for instance.

[Here follows the note from Gerrit's mother, with one line from his father, which Hilde refers to in this letter]

Dear Gerrit,

We were happy to read your letter, very very happy, but please be sure not to become reckless. This is the first time we heard from you. Pleased with parcel. We did get several small parcels of butter and cheese from the lady friend while still permitted but now only one package @ 2 kg is allowed every four weeks. Good news from Suze. Love from your mother. We are trying to stay healthy. Are well at the moment. In haste.

Lots of kisses and a big hug from your Dad

Friday evening, January 7, 1944

Dear Gait,

Well, I decided to start scribbling again, in hopes that this will once more reach you promptly. Last night I had to finish in a hurry again, but then, I was really too tired to go on writing anyway. One of the symptoms of hepatitis is that one doesn't have much energy, so I sleep quite a bit during the day, especially as there are frequent interruptions during the night. The care we get here is as good as can be expected in a place like this, so I consider myself very lucky that I need very little help from the nurses for they really have their hands full with patients who are more critically ill and more demanding. Moreover there are many unlicensed nurses here, some quite unsuitable individuals among them (and among the licensed nurses as well).

Perhaps you would enjoy hearing that the head nurse on our ward is a very sweet and extremely capable woman who reminds me very strongly, in her features as well as in her gestures and behavior down to some of the smallest details, of your sister Jo, a fact which endears her even more to me of course. As you know, there are more than a hundred patients on the ward, so the ward was subdivided into three sections, each headed by a nurse in charge, and imagine what a pleasant coincidence that the nurse in charge of my area, the hepatitis section, is Sophietje Cohen from Delft who was the director of Beth Refoeah for a long time, do you remember? On the Hooge Naarderweg, at the upper end of the Insulindeweg. I know we also saw her once or twice at Nathan's, and in addition she nursed me at the Fransche Laan, I believe it was in 1935. She is a real dear and I enjoy spoiling her from time to time, which unfortunately I can only do on rare occasions. But I could not resist popping a small piece of the chocolate into her mouth and also having her take home a piece for her one-and-a-half year old daughter.

Willy Polak often stops by in the evening for a short chat, which I enjoy greatly. He does not really come to see me, to tell you the truth, but a cousin of his whose bed happens to be next to mine. He often comes by the ward because his eighty-eight year old mother is confined here. She is not ill, but too old for the barracks, so she lives here, so to speak, which he managed to arrange for her. The mother also stops by often for a chat on her daily rounds; she is the epitome of a charming elderly lady. It is fun to see her lending a hand to everyone who is not allowed out of bed, frying potatoes and eggs on the stove, and making herself useful in every way.

Perhaps you wonder why I am not in a small hospital barrack, but the hepatitis patients were expressly assigned to this one. I estimate that there are close to a hundred hepatitis patients here, counting men and women. Among them is Werner Diamant, Big Bram's son-in-law, and I was told that he truly looks green and that he, too, has been down with this for several weeks already.

Now I want to tell you of a curious coincidence, which is that in my first few days in the hospital I had as my neighbor a sister of Joseph [. . .]. He and his brother have unfortunately already moved on as far as I know, and this woman has British papers [. . .] probably leave with many others this coming Tuesday [. . .] concentration camp Zelle near Hannover.

Many people on the Palestine lists will have to leave too, and to my great sorrow Otto is among them. Of course this is supposed to be preferential treatment, but no one is leaving with enthusiasm, to put it mildly. So everyone is hoping that something will interfere at the last moment, as it did on November 23.

I had a lovely surprise this afternoon when Otto came by on a surreptitious visit. He just popped in to bring me some bottles of soda water, the spoils of an intensive hunt. Knowing my taste, you'll realize I didn't just flip, I did a triple flip of course. The things that can make a person happy nowadays!

By the way, I just want to say that you must not think I am pitifully miserable. You know that I manage to adjust to almost any situation; especially when I know that there are no alternatives, I try to make the best of it. Otherwise it would long since have become unbearable. I try not to reflect; that is absolutely futile, and I cannot envision any plans for the future at all at the moment. I just float, at least for the time being.

I would like to know, however, how your friend is

planning to play Saint Nicolas; please let me know some more about that, if at all possible. But I stand firm in my concern about the parents, although that will probably no longer be a concern by the time I have recovered from this lengthy illness. As soon as I am back in my regular barrack again we [. . .] take another look at this matter. There is no sense for you to continue speculating about this matter either right now. I am sorry that you were already waiting for a visit from Mouse a long time ago, and I can imagine your disappointment when she did not come. But in my opinion Jan and Jack tend to take these things too lightly, just as Dé's counselors were much too naive in his case.

Your parents are really doing very well, except for the fact that your father is also in Ward 6 with a heavy cold, as you must have heard. In the meantime he has improved considerably and he gets good care. They live in Barrack 42 and each of them has a good bottom bunk. Their barrack leader is Mrs. Bachrach from the Dalweg, and of course I made her promise to take good care of them. They are well provided with all the necessities. Father's rubber boots and Mother's sewing supplies came along too, even yarn and knitting needles, so she already knitted him a nice new scarf after he had lost his.

It is not so surprising, is it, that we did not leave any of our luggage with Horst, for there really was no reason to do so when we were released for the second time. In the distant past he once managed to get me a beautiful piece of veal for the meat ration cards!!!

Never heard or saw anything of Eva and Harry Citters. Ab Coronel and Aal, Dr. K., and about all the others came with me, but most of them on a tour of duty which is being extended all the time, most recently until January 31. Every now and then one of them is here for a day or two, and thus we are expecting Bernhard [. . .] here tomorrow.

Dr. K's wife received an "S" about two months ago!! But she is out again as of yesterday! Fortunately [. . .]

Mrs. Weismann also got rid of her "S" stamp and she'll

leave with her little son on the "Blue Train" on Tuesday (this refers to the category of blue stamps, as you have probably understood.) She has been lying in a bed across from me for the past three weeks, but wants to travel regardless; she is doing quite well anyway. The length of this illness varies from three or four weeks to... fifteen weeks and more. Anneliese Lederer was sick with it for sixteen weeks, no less, so I may have a while to go yet!

Now I have digressed totally from Otto's surreptitious visit, and I had intended to tell you that he stayed with me for at least an hour and a half without being told to leave even then. As there were practically no other visitors on the ward, it was wonderfully quiet and we could have a very long and relaxed talk together. Who knows when we'll be able to do this again??

He really has recovered from Bella, although she clings to him faithfully; but he pays no attention anymore. The relationship with Bé is pleasant and cordial. She works in the toy workshop, painting toys, and Herta works at the Herzberg Studio. Both look well and come to visit me from time to time. They work long hours of course, and especially Bé has many patients to visit. Besides Daan, there is Heleen and her little son who was operated on his ear. I read Otto parts of your letters, which I thought was all right to do. He was so grateful and showed such warm empathy. He also loved your poem and the letter from Yoka.

I had planned to continue writing tomorrow but must stop now for the usual reason. Hope to write again soon.

A thousand kisses,
Hilde

Stay well and take care

Of all things! I totally forgot to mention that all shipments arrived promptly and that I am very grateful: wonderful eggs, one of which I had someone fry right away, black bread, and lovely apples today. I am utterly grateful for everything. H.

[Wednesday] January 12, [1944]

It took a few more days until I could get around to writing you again, and in the meantime there have been great changes here, for—hold on tight—not only did Otto leave yesterday, but also, and utterly unexpectedly, Selma and Paul. It was especially unpleasant that they were not notified until nine-thirty the night before, just imagine, so that they had to make all the arrangements and pack everything the next morning. But you know what an energetic and courageous darling Selma is, and you can imagine that they had to beat off, so to speak, all the people who wanted to help them. I haven't heard any details of their leaving yet but I hope to get a full report from Clara tomorrow at visiting hours.

Monday afternoon Selma was still here to see me, faithful as always, for she never missed an opportunity to show up with some tasty surprise. At that time she did not have an inkling yet. So you can begin to imagine my utter shock when I received a note from Selma and Paul with the news and a goodbye message on Tuesday morning. I was totally dazed, and very sad that I could not be with her for help and support. Perhaps it was a good thing that we did not have to say goodbye face to face, and as to their future fate, I hope and trust that their lucky stars will once more protect them. Under the circumstances, perhaps we may feel fairly confident about this trip. I myself have high hopes of it, at least as much as or perhaps even more than of Theresienstadt. Also, in this transport they had a lot of company, and I like to think that they and Otto were able to give each other mutual support and assistance. I don't know if they traveled together but I suppose not. Otto probably went with his friends, and Selma and Paul surely had enough good company from our barrack, Chief Rabbi Davids among them, and many other nice families who all liked them very much.

I had got this far with my story two weeks ago, when I suddenly heard that our little blond friend was also planning to move against his will. I had been very surprised at the fact that he had not been in to see me at all after the *eleventh*, and I am actually quite curious to hear whether Wim had still spoken to him after that date.

On that day there was an incident here involving someone who was transporting something similar to F., and at first I thought that had given him cold feet, and that that was the reason why he didn't come to see me anymore. By the way, Fie and E's old neighbor, the friend of your parents, got burned fairly badly with an "S" in the process, but he is still here fortunately and possibly may get away with the scare, bad as it was. Unfortunately I do not have any more details, as I'm still confined to bed.

Yes, you may be surprised to hear that I am still lying in bed, and not making much headway. Apparently, I also do this very slowly and thoroughly, like everything else, and after eight weeks—it's unbelievable—I still look quite yellow. At one point it seemed to improve, but then returned with a vengeance. I got much more jaundiced than the first time; they call it "recidivism" which speaks for itself. It seems to be fairly common, even after patients have been discharged from the hospital as cured. It happens that some come back after one or two weeks looking saffron-yellow, and have to start all over again. The doctor very kindly and consolingly tells me that I have no right to complain until it has been four months, so I may have something in store for me yet.

Let me tell you though that I don't feel ill at all and that my appetite is excellent (unfortunately, considering the meager rations!). The inevitable consequence of being confined to bed for so long is considerable weakening of course, but apparently that will improve quickly once you're up and about again.

I sleep a great deal and luckily my cough is much bet-

ter, so that I sleep better at night. But while I sleep I per-
spire very heavily, it's really awful, and I find it extremely
unpleasant. The doctor claims that this is also caused by the
hepatitis, but since it is getting worse and worse I am very
much afraid it is also a sign of weakening. And that is me,
who for the past twenty years never spent a day in bed except three times for happy reasons.

In the meantime I had been on the lookout eagerly
after G's departure on the 18th, because I was convinced
that you and Wim would not be sitting still. When it took
so long I was just planning to sound out Horst, but at that
very moment things started to move again, to my very great
joy, as you can imagine. True, Bernhard came in to see me
once in the meantime, but he never has time to give any details and anyway, getting news from him was not the same
at all.

I was very happy with all the good news and especially
all the other things were also very much appreciated. My
cupboard had been totally bare for a few weeks because I
had told Selma and Paul to use what little stock I had. I also
divided the oatmeal and sugar which I had received from Lé
just prior to their departure among those who were leaving.
The only thing I kept for myself was a quarter of the cheese,
and I must say, I managed quite well, even though I really
could have eaten a lot more than four slices of bread in the
morning and evening. But then, as soon as you do get something, you cannot leave it alone and you attack it hungrily.
Thus I allowed myself the luxury of eating a hard-boiled
egg last night, which was a delicious treat, just that I could
have managed to eat several slices of bread with it! Being
confined to my hospital bed, I really do not have a chance to
scrounge around for bread, and our parents are not resourceful enough to do so. Unfortunately, the rations canteen was closed down after the incident involving Fie's
neighbor, so that I could not use the bread ration coupons
which I still had. I then continued my supper with the
apple, and I am ashamed to admit that I helped myself to

some honey several times last night. It certainly will not last long, for it is much too good and of course also quite beneficial for my cough.

Our parents were terribly pleased today with the lovely surprise, and I gave part of the honey to your mother to take to Father. He is still hospitalized and unfortunately not yet allowed to get up.

Your mother is really very brave and strong, and she looks very well. She was very happy with the good news, and the other things were manna from heaven of course. The bread situation is quite miserable for most people here, but if they have a bit of butter they can fry some potatoes every now and then. You sent us a large amount all at once, perhaps you didn't know that Paul and Selma were gone. I do have to confess though that we can use all sorts of things, especially now that my appetite, which was so minimal during the first stage of my illness, has returned with a vengeance. I do not know if you can arrange all this, but especially bread, also black bread, honey cake, cheese, oatmeal, sugar cubes, and biscuits are most welcome. But don't send too much at one time, because of possible difficulties in getting it here. Am I very demanding? But I really am very hungry, after having eaten hardly anything for six weeks and then everything I could lay my hands on, which wasn't very much, for the past two. Your mother would be terribly happy with a pound of white beans and a few onions to make a pot of soup some time. Perhaps it is possible to provide her with these, also some vermicelli!

Now I shall start answering your letters. Had I expressed my admiration yet for the wonderful farming poem?[2] It was very good and I am sure Yoka enjoyed it.

The other day I had with great effort printed a very good, very long letter to Frankie, but unfortunately Bernhard did not dare to take it, and instead of returning it to me so I could send it another time, he destroyed it! How wonderful that you had such a nice cart made for Otto, only when shall we see him in it? I am constantly looking for five-year-old boys, to see how big he must be by now. In a bottom bunk next to me there is a nine-year-old girl who reminds me of Evelientje Gottlieb.[3] She has a six-year-old brother in the men's ward with hepatitis who is almost well. He often visits his sister, for he is allowed to get up and walk around, and sometimes they eat their evening meal here together, so then I can observe him to my heart's content, and then, how my thoughts wander. . . . Last night, Friday night, it was so sweet to see how they had set a festive Sabbath table. He was sitting at the foot of the bed, and in between them on a towel everything had been neatly set out; even the salt for the blessing had not been forgotten and he gravely handed the bread to his sister after having first dipped it properly into the salt!

[Sunday, January 30]

I had gotten up to this point last night (Saturday) when I wrote from ten to twelve midnight, for I was afraid that I would be too tired to write again today and indeed I am glad I did, because I can still get on with a job much better at night than during the day, same as ever. Since there is always a weak light burning here all night anyway, it went very well. Only my fountain pen is on the blink and that slows me down a lot. So I switched over to dipping it in the ink each time, but that takes a lot more ink, and I don't know where I am going to get new ink when this bottle is finished. I don't like to write in pencil, because that gets so messy and takes even more paper, and I have already had to scrounge around for these pages, for my note pad is finished. I do have another in my luggage somewhere, but I have to figure out first who is to dig it out for me. I'll see if Clara can do it. She was in to see me several times after Selma and Paul's departure, very caring, and every time she brought me something good to eat, a little pudding, or a cup of tea or some grated carrots or something, to continue

Selma's tradition. Of course she told me all about their departure in great detail, and she sobbed so uncontrollably that it could not have been worse if her own mother had left. Fortunately Selma and Paul were well supplied with everything; you can imagine how bravely that dear Selma packed everything and it is unbelievable what food Clara still managed to give to them: two whole loaves of bread and two loaves of black bread which she had just brought from the canteen, which was still open then, plus half a tin of biscuits, a beautiful box of chocolates (Peppie and Grietje insisted that they take it) and I don't know what else. Selma had packed everything in that beautiful big canister and tied it securely, and thus they carried their precious food between the two of them. It is terribly sad of course that there is no way of finding out how they have fared so far, and will fare from now on, and my thoughts wander off to them quite often. At any rate they traveled in a real people train and according to [. . .] the consensus is that the people on this transport have the best chance of all of those who have departed so far.

There is a lot of talk at the moment of an imminent departure of the 120,000, also to Zelle near Hannover, but that is still very uncertain. If it should come to that, I really cannot do a thing about it, and neither can R.A. nor anyone else. I never heard anything about that business which Siem had planned to arrange for Theresienstadt, nor whether your parents received a letter from him, which they surely would have told me. Another thing is that no one here can say whether Zelle is to be preferred over Theresienstadt or the other way around. Moreover I think they will let your father stay here for the time being until he has recovered, so I suppose we can just let things rest for the moment.

The question of where my parents will end up remains wide open too. In case of departure of the 120,000, they could probably remain here a little longer, if they so desire, because of their Callmeyer situation, but there is a large risk involved, because if that list should fail, then of course they risk Poland. So it is fraught with problems and complications, as you can see. If the Callmeyer list holds, I want you to know that in my case a divorce wouldn't do any good, since I was married to a Jew on the cutoff date, which was January 1, 1942, if I am not mistaken.

I want to say again that you must not be too sad that you cannot do more for me, because you are really doing an awful lot, and I know that you are not sitting idly by. In addition, you've had so many things to organize for the trio, and that need will go on. The main thing is that all may stay healthy and that the present situation may remain stable as long as that is necessary; then I would be content and utterly grateful!

I have always been aware of the fact that Wim is such a terrific fellow and his wife too, and I am terribly grateful to them for everything they are doing for me and our parents. Please make sure however that they, too, *remain* careful and don't do anything foolish. Anyway, I don't understand his intentions at all regarding the closing of that deal for your 50 percent, and it would be a good idea if you, who know the local situation, could give me some more information. Should all the luggage just be left behind, or is there another possibility?

Hugo, Lenie's husband, came over last week after his return from Amsterdam to bring me very special greetings from Roelie, who also seemed to have good stuff for Wim. It might be useful for Wim to go and see him some time, I believe his address is Singel 93.

Bernhard brought me a note from Frankie the other day, but unfortunately it was again not one she had written independently, so it wasn't much fun. Bernhard has seen her several times now and is very much taken with her. He assured me that she has developed beautifully and that she plays the piano very sweetly. Did you know that? Did you manage to find out what happened to that lovely little coat which I had delivered that Wednesday morning at #12, the home of your old boss? You wrote that you managed to get

Signs of Life

new overalls for Otto! I had never stopped to think about the fact that those lovely new overalls and those lovely sweaters had stayed behind too, together with all the many, many irreplaceable things! That man Siem really is an idiot! Think of how much could have been salvaged in one night. Well, there is nothing we can do about it now.

If you wish to get anything from Sporw. for Dé, that can probably only be arranged through Emmy with Marie of the corks. Emmy lives at Minervaplein 14 (??).

You asked about diapers for Wim, but that may be difficult, because I used them to wrap the good china in. You were right about To Scholz. Orchideestraat 9. But I foresee lots of problems. Perhaps it would be a good idea to contact Corrie v. Abs, Eikenlaan 25, for help.

As regards the poor arrangements for packages, it is true that the parents of the boys took care of that together, and did the best they could in their way, but once a week or even less was of course painfully little for the two of them together and it would have been no luxury if Siem et al. had sent at least as much again. But they are totally uncaring and insensitive anyway, in their bourgeois complacency. What mattered most to them was that they had covered themselves and "were making sure that others were doing it" so they didn't have to give it another thought. Even if Father and Mother had been receiving a wealth of things from others, it still would not have been amiss to send something too every now and then, as a kind gesture. But they can in any case go to hell as far as I am concerned, and always could, for as long as I've known them!! No need to respond to this.

As far as packages are concerned, the discussion is closed; and as for Siem and his cohorts, let him ride on the coattails of M[o] W[olff], but please don't you get tempted to do the same. Rather strike out on your own, which you are quite capable of. And I want to help you with that as much as I can, when we are together again!!!

I have another piece of news for you, namely that

Michel was relieved of "S" status and apparently has a solid exemption. I don't know any more about it, but they certainly are still here, don't worry!

Unfortunately, the mother of little Finy Gersons arrived here with her sister after a year and a half, and both of them moved on. I was very upset and I also think so often of poor Rudi and Finy with their darling children. I wonder how they are??

Berthold now lives in #64 also, where my parents are. And Finy is still as lazy and greedy as ever. She wouldn't even give Mother a drop of vinegar for a salad!! I believe that Father and Mother used to treat them very differently in the past. In the eight weeks that I have been in the hospital Berthold has been in to see me all of one time, and Finy never; not surprisingly, Henri is still as sloppy and filthy as he used to be. If she knew that I still have a good supply of cigarettes, she would come running, I'm sure. So you see the story of "The Dog that Barked" is still quite to the point: nothing has changed and nothing will change in people's character.

It's getting to be time to conclude this letter. I am surprised at myself, that I had enough energy to put in another two hours of writing, but the result is that a bead of perspiration is suspended from every single hair on my head, and I could swim in my bed. Yet it was no strain but a great pleasure to be able to talk to you at such length. I hope to be able to write again soon, for I'm not through talking with you yet, and I know that you are a captive audience now that you don't have to listen to me! Or have you got more patience for that these days?

Stay well, dear Gait, and I hope to get a long letter from you again very soon.

I fully expect to have writer's cramp tomorrow.

A thousand heartfelt kisses from *Mouse* (the cool gray one)

[Additions in the margins]

Warmest regards to Wim and his wife and warmest thanks for all their kind support!

Shall I return those ration coupons to you next time? Or do they stay valid? In that case I'd like to keep them here just in case. Could you also send me some plain bouillon cubes please, to make a cup of soup.

I still have a lot to write next time—can you believe it?

[Monday] January 31, [1944]

My Dear Gait,

Here comes an addition since this letter will be sent a day later than planned, for there were no visiting hours last night (Sunday), which we had not taken into account when we made our arrangements. And to compensate you for the longer wait, I feel obliged to bore you with at least one more page. I would spare you the ordeal if it weren't for the fact that a whole laundry list of items for discussion popped into my head in the meantime. Item no. 1 is the matter of the Weinreb list which seems to have been reopened for applications. I agree with you entirely that so far no one has ever actually seen any good come from these lists, but that is precisely why it might have been extremely useful if you would have had the matter checked out on the outside by Mo or Jack. Siem probably would not have moved a finger in this case either. At least your parents never received a letter such as you describe, with a special designation for Theresienstadt on the grounds of having connections abroad. It is possible of course that the total mail stop since January 11 delayed the letter. That could be. At any rate, your parents received a summons yesterday for tomorrow's transport to Zelle, which of course shook them up considerably and especially your mother was very angry that Mo had not arranged better protection for them, whereas the Broekmans and Renée Wolff do have such a special deferment arranged by him, so that they do not have to worry about deportation yet. You know how very indignant she can get in a situation like that, whereas it is not clear at all yet what may be in store for the Broekmans and the W[olff]s.

Another reason for her to dread the prospect of the trip was that Father is still in the hospital, so she would have had to handle everything by herself. I immediately sent my father and later also Willy Polak to his attending physician (Zwaap from Hilversum), who had already certified him unfit for transport, so I can be sure that they are safe for tomorrow, insofar as one can be sure of anything here. Your mother dropped in again for her usual visit this morning, clearly much relieved and calmer; but she is still of course very upset that Mo didn't do the same for them as he had done for the Broekmans and the W[olff]s.

It appears that my parents are not going to be summoned for this transport, probably because of their Callmeyer situation which is still limping along. Anyway, let's hope it will continue to limp along for a long time yet and to a happy ending.

By the way, you should try to get in touch with Lé once more to ask him if he doesn't have a good connection at Callmeyer's who can advocate and expedite Ber and Dé's case. I seem to remember him writing me something to that effect, although his own mother's case is not moving very expeditiously either: she has been here for almost a year now and her case is still not quite resolved. I must say that Lé really has done an awful lot for me, and I especially cherish his frequent warm and caring letters. He also promptly arranged a parcel when the so-called parcel rule prevailed, and once he had W Z brought to me, all paid for out of his own pocket, including all the care packages. He is truly too good for this world, reason perhaps why things are not going too well for him personally.

Lotte still writes long nostalgic letters, but in my opinion it will still take a good long time before we'll see her and all the others again, in spite of all the silly talk of Lena Lieberg's neighbors![4]

Now I've totally digressed from the Weinreb list, but I suggest you make inquiries into the matter. Since I agree with you in principle about export in the wrong direction, I won't do anything about it here until I get more information from you. I am definitely interested in Wim's plans eventually, especially when my current objections will have been removed, but first I'll have to be altogether better and back in my own barrack, and that may take another six weeks, for my case is a very protracted one. We've found that out already! Old Dr. Lek often comes over for a chat, and he always tries to comfort me about the length of my illness, and so does Coenraad Heymans, the little captain/surgeon! Do you remember that we took him to the Oranje Nassau barracks one evening? Dr. Weyl from Middelburg who used to live with the Vaz Diaz family also stops to chat whenever he happens to be on my ward, so I get plenty of entertainment at my bedside.

Moreover I have a very nice neighbor who has been here for more than eight weeks, by the way, and a few beds down is Druyf's wife (she is Bram's sister-in-law, I believe, at any rate not the Druyfs who used to come visit us on their tandem bike sometimes). I recognized her from the time we both stayed in the same hotel in Zandvoort, twenty years ago. Her son, now twenty-five, and safe and sound in Amsterdam because of a mixed marriage, was a toddler at the time, same age as Yoka was when we were in Zandvoort four years ago, and he had a similar exclusive tricycle, which in those days was something really special. This memory has always stayed with me because at the time someone took a particularly nice photo of all the children staying at the hotel lined up by height with their bicycles, including me, with my German bike! Perhaps I'll be able to show you that picture some day!

I could still go on chatting with you, but I'll stop now, otherwise you'll never ever dare to write me again! If you like, I could write a *short* letter some time! What a collection of nonsense this has gotten to be.

Well, dearest, take care and keep your spirits up. Warm regards to Wim and his wife, also to Jan and Jack.

A thousand kisses to you.

H.

[Additions in the margins]

Dear Gait, I am to give you warmest regards and love from your parents and also many thanks for all you sent them. I had told them to write you a few words themselves, but they said they'd rather not.

Kind regards also from my parents and many thanks. Please don't forget the bouillon cubes; they make such a nice 11 a.m. treat!

Hiemso family is definitely going to Zelle tomorrow, but without S. That's still very lucky.

Notes

1. Johan Dank was Gerrit's uncle who was married to his mother's sister Nanette (Nette). He was not Jewish and had died before the war.
2. Gerrit had written a very amusing rhymed description of his activities as a new farmhand in his hiding place.
3. Evelientje Gottlieb was Yoka's friend. She and her mother were German refugees; both were killed during the war.
4. Helena Lieberg-Stibbe, the sister-in-law of Caroline Stibbe-Verdoner, Gerrit's sister, who lived near London. By "neighbors" Hilde possibly means "the British."

Hilde's last note, written in pencil to her father on February 7, 1944, the eve of her deportation.

David Sluizer   [February 7, 1944]

Barrack 64

Dear Father,

   My worst fears have been realized and I have been called up for transport.

   Do what you can!

   I have very little hope.

   Stay healthy and strong.

   Send me a note back as soon as possible if you find out anything.

A thousand kisses
Hilde

Eyewitness report of Hilde's transport.

Wednesday, February 9 [1944]

Yesterday's transport of the sick from the hospital barracks to the train defies all description. At two in the morning, nurses began to dress patients who had been selected for transport. Men of the Special Service, driving open, horse-drawn carts, shoved the sick on their stretchers onto the carts, next to and on top of each other, as though shoving so many coffins into a hearse. In the dark winter morning, wet snow dripped from the dark skies, covering everything with a sticky, damp, white film. That is how they were driven to the cattle train, jolting and bumping in the carts. Then they lay there out in the open, waiting to be loaded, as corpses are loaded into a hearse. . . . Of all the transports that have left here, perhaps this was the most bestial.

From Philip Mechanicus, *In Dépôt*, p. 276.

Epilogue

Hildegard Verdoner-Sluizer was deported from Westerbork on February 8, 1944. She died in Auschwitz on February 11, 1944, at the age of thirty-four.

Otto Sluizer was deported from Westerbork on January 11, 1944. He died in Bergen Belsen on January 9, 1945, at the age of thirty-three.

David and Bertha Sluizer were deported from Westerbork on February 25, 1944, to Theresienstadt. Both survived and returned to their home at Reynier Vinkeleskade 73 in Amsterdam. David died in 1964, at the age of eighty-eight; Bertha died in 1966, at the age of eighty-eight.

Paul and Selma Wallman were deported from Westerbork on January 11, 1944. Paul died in Bergen Belsen on December 24, 1944, at the age of sixty-nine. Selma died in Bergen Belsen on May 24, 1945, five and a half weeks after the camp was liberated on April 15, 1945. She was sixty-four.

Abraham and Henriette Verdoner were deported from Westerbork on February 8, 1944. They died in Auschwitz on February 11, 1944. Both of them were seventy-four years of age.

References

Boas, Jacob. *Boulevard des Misères: The Story of Transit Camp Westerbork*. (Hamden, Connecticut: Archon Books, 1985).

Hillesum, Etty. *Letters from Westerbork*. Translated from the Dutch by Arnold J. Pomerans. (New York: Pantheon Books, 1986).

Mechanicus, Philip. *In Dépôt: Dagboek uit Westerbork*. (Amsterdam: Polak & van Gennep, 1964).

-----. *Year of Fear. A Jewish Prisoner Waits for Auschwitz.* (Edited translation of *In Dépôt.*) Translated from the Dutch by Irene S. Gibbons. (New York: 1968).

Presser, Jacob. *Ashes in the Wind:The Destruction of Dutch Jewry.* Translated from the Dutch by Arnold J. Pomerans. (Detroit: Wayne State University Press, 1988).

The original letters are on deposit at the Netherlands State Institute for War Documentation (Rijksinstituut voor Oorlogsdocumentatie) in Amsterdam.

Westerbork today.